Where Yellow Ribbon Daffodils Grow

Where Yellow Ribbon Daffodils Grow

Robert A. DeJesus

To order additional copies of this book, contact:
Xlibris
844-714-8691
www.Xlibris.com
Orders@Xlibris.com
826107

Contents

WRITING

NATURE

RELIGION

LOVE

LOSS

WOUNDED

MISCELLANEOUS PERSPECTIVES/PHILOSOPHIES

SONG FOR GENE

AN APPRECIATION OF LIFE

To my wife, Alysa, for her relentless love, support, inspiration, and patience.

To my children—Brandee, Andrew, Jacob, Jordyn, and Joshua—for the honor and privilege of being your father and for filling my life with pride and laughter.

To my mother, Alma, who provided the unconditional love every child deserves.

To Cara Fillmore, for her genius, guidance, and generosity.

Writing

Ideas

"Poetry = touch" on subtle but human interactions. Make up for the lack of inflection or tone from a singer's voice with the exact words that express a precise feeling or humanness. Describe that which is often taken for granted but is a critical piece of information that often gives context to the situation or circumstance being described.

Take chances with word arrangements, challenge the status quo styles of yesteryear, and have fun making your ideas gleam from a different perspective. Be courageous, loud, and exaggerative. Be simple, clear, and communicative.

Allow yourself the freedom to touch yourself in places you've never dared to explore. Most of all, poetry is about feeling. It invokes the opportunity to become one with your own emotions, and it allows for the chance to become enlightened to the doors you were always afraid to open.

Poetry touches everyone on an individual level. Write for yourself and be true to your feelings, and you will find that you are not alone. That which is most dear to you may only scratch the surface of another, and the reverse is true as well. Your least favorite piece might gain the greatest recognition.

Humanity is poetry. Poetry is timeless.

1998–2002

My Voice

You want to know if I have a voice, if I have something to say?

Let me tell you something . . . I have my thoughts. I have my moments. There are times when you can't shut me up. Even when you think I've stopped, I've only really just begun. My voice speaks volumes to nobody but me. You may never hear a word my voice says, but I promise you, it's talking, telling me about its perception of everything it sees, feels, and hears and also its perception of its perception of those things.

You know, sometimes I even get tired of my voice. Sometimes my voice just won't let things go. If I could shut it up, then maybe I'd get more sleep at night. At times, my voice likes to repeat things over and over—you know, like some dumb song it's heard or the final words someone or anyone has expressed. It drives me crazy. Believe me, listening to you is entertainment to me. It gives me the chance to rest for the moment—but only for the moment 'cause listening to you only gets my voice going again.

You see, my vocal cords were amputated when I was a child, cut clean through my adolescent years. At times, I thought they were sprouting new roots, but I was firmly reminded. Then one day my voice grabbed a pen and scrawled some gibberish on a piece of paper. I wasn't sure why, but it felt good. It began to talk about everything and anything it wanted. It had an opinion! That was scary.

I was unsure if I should let anyone know about this voice. What would they think, and should I give ownership to this voice? It spoke a language that I understood. It expressed itself like I would. The strange thing about it was the more I wrote, the more I learned to admire it. Also, I found that allowing it to write was a good way to get some sleep . . . sometimes.

My voice was definitely unique, but at times, I wasn't sure if it had been listening to some old tapes of my parents to get its ideas. Eventually, I began to trust my voice. Then I began to share it with others. It took some time—lots of time, *years*—and at times, I still hesitate to expose it to others.

However, just in case anyone asks you about that quiet guy sitting over there, go ahead and tell them, "Yeah, he has a voice."

March 17, 1999

Poetry

It's really not that difficult.
Well, then again, it does take time.
I start out with some passion,
Nothing really by design.

Then I grab the pen and paper
And ask myself how I feel.
Sometimes the words spill right out.
Other times, it's not so real.

Soon, I'll have a stanza or two
On which I'd like to build.
I'll dig a little deeper
'Til all the lines are filled.

I guess it's fair to say
The tough parts are the words.
I try to choose them carefully
To make sure each thought is heard.

Finally, I bend the phrases
Up and down and inside out
'Til the ideas are like a puzzle
But the message leaves no doubt.
February 2, 1998

Creativity

I woke today with not much to say,
Though creativity was alive.
It pressed against my inner being
Until it forced my thoughts to contrive.

At first, I confess, I drew a blank,
Not knowing where it wanted to flow.
So I squished it in and pushed it back,
Tried to plan for a day on the go.

As I drove to work, I felt it twist
And knew it had made up its mind.
It wasn't about to just give in,
For you see, it's not merely that kind.

I turned up the music to counter,
Though in the past, it was futile indeed.
In due time, I always surrendered
To its hunger and relentless need.

My resistance began to weaken
As by now, its hands had become free.
It began to touch and probe my thoughts,
Causing a turmoil inside of me.

I knew giving in would ease my pain
As it slowly invaded my pores.

My every thought soon focused on it.
With my walls down, I opened the doors.

It flooded my goals and direction.
I abandoned the calendar day,
Set out to appease my true master
In the effort to keep him at bay.

I learned his plight was symbiotic,
For his success was really my gain,
And the struggle and battle within
Disappeared 'til we raised arms again.
September 22, 1999

Shape of Words

Some brag of words with rounded ends
That flow along like river bends,
Smooth as silk, rolling off your tongue,
Soft as lullabies warmly sung.
Simply say the word *bubble gum*.
You'll see its shape is like a plum.

By contrast, there's a clamorous clan,
Creating terms just because they can,
With the contours sharp and cutting clean,
Distinct as the corners of a skein.
Try to speak the term *cantankerous*.
Triangles can be quite dangerous.

Still, there are some that mix the two,
With words that stick to one like glue,
Like *caramel, cotton candy,*
Ice cream cones, and *chocolate* can be.
Though similar, they share no shape,
Instead seem destined to escape.
November 24, 1999

Passion

To want to breathe it,
Whatever it might be.
To want to live in it—
It's the only thing you see.
To want to taste it,
Savor every last drop.
To want to feel it
And never want to stop.
To want to bathe in it,
Immerse your heart and soul.
To glow within it
As it's your only goal.
To anticipate it
With every second on the clock.
To defend it,
Firm and solid as a rock.
To long and yearn for it
When it's not around.
To feel a void without it
When you have to set it down.
To live without it
Would be a very mournful day.
To have never known it—
I can't imagine life that way.
September 12, 1998

Passion For

It's your rush. It's your happiness.
It's your lover. It's your friend.
It's your reason for living.
It's your peace in the end.

It's your drive. It's your motivator.
It's your blood. It's your being.
It's your every waking thought.
It's the fantasy you're dreaming.

It's your pain. It's your agony.
It's your failures. It's your success.
It's your never-ending strife.
It's the reason for your quest.
September 12, 1998

The Book

The book has long been written as a mark of history.

The tales are short and lengthy within each story.

The chapters are only segments to separate the plans.

The pages are numerically ordered to refer to on command.

The paragraphs give one clues to continue with the race.

The lines are lonely statements created to fill the space.

The words are selected carefully so that we comprehend.

The letters are the essence to what is called "the end."

May 23, 1986

Introspection

For some, there is no more difficult an assessment
than that discovered behind the pen.

March 17, 1998

Nature

The Poet's Seasons

The poet's seasons don't taste the same.
Each feels of a different flavor.
When you touch their words,
You can smell their texture.
When they paint the air,
You can hear their colors,
And when they scream out loud,
You can sense their silence,

For you will see their pictures
As if you were blind.

Close your eyes.

The poet's seasons don't feel the same,
A spring of green rivers through your veins,
Fertile soil bathes on your palate,
A single bird . . .

Broken silence of winter's tomb.
Reborn to experience—
Alive.

The poet's seasons don't sound the same.
A shaded spot hides summer's flame.

Afternoons breathe slow and long.
The flies . . .

Buzzing mowers clip spring away—
A time for napping.
Recline.

The poet's seasons don't smell the same.
Yesterday covers autumn's roads.
Gloom colors the sky with clouds.
Yellow and black buses . . .

Summer waves to us goodbye.
A reflective smile—
Alone.

The poet's seasons don't look the same.
Tomorrow sleeps 'neath winter's coat.
Almond logs will pop and glow.
Chimneys . . .

Puffing autumn's dying breath.
Hibernation—
Still.

The poet's seasons don't taste the same.

October 13, 1999

The View

I took a drive one afternoon
Upon a gravel road, but soon,
The road wound up and back and forth
'Til east was west and south felt north.

The sound of rocks all disappeared,
And dirt replaced the dust that cleared.
I found myself atop the peak.
Consumed with awe, I couldn't speak.

The view below was such a sight
Of twinkling shards reflecting light.
The summer's sun, which brushed my face,
Caressed my soul with its embrace.

The distant rooftops set in rows
Concealed the chaos and our woes,
Instead appeared as we had planned—
As harmony across the land.

The golden hills danced in the breeze,
Which passed like waves on through the trees.
It called the birds, who perched inside
And sang their freedom song with pride.

I still recall the lack of noise,
The peaceful calm, the wild squirrels' poise.

They stopped a bit to look and stare
And sniff the scent of summer's air.

The sun then spoke its will to sleep
But left behind for me to keep
A painted sky of vibrant hues,
Of orange reds and purple blues.

The silhouette across the bay
Of sculpted mountains cut away
Suggest a beauty so unknown,
I contemplate we're not alone.

I turned to take one final gaze,
Pause for the moment with just praise,
Thought reflectively as I returned
The precious lesson I had learned.

I found the road back home had cleared
Without the twists and turns I feared,
And so I came to understand
A view is formed by where you stand.

February 8, 1999

Rain on the Asphalt

Don't you recall that smell?

Steam rises as the raindrops turn the gray streets to black.
Slowly, the runoff meets the gutters, beginning its long journey to the sea.

That smell—you know, the one that comes with its promise to cleanse the air—
Yet the scent it gives off is not entirely pleasant.

It's the one that reminds you that the season is changing; the sky takes on a darker shade, and the winds gain a little more strength.

That smell almost carries a weight of its own.
Mentally, you somehow share and feel the burden of that weight.

For that brief instant, you feel the powerful influence of nature.
Time stops upon the recognition of that smell, and with that pause, it demands to be acknowledged.
You stand in a haze, momentarily suspended while you contemplate all that is, has been, and will be . . .

Ask any kid. They'll tell you. They know that smell.
It means the first day of school is just around the corner.
It means homework, teachers, and tests,
Crammed school buses with condensation dripping down the windows.

It signifies a change in not only your mood but your wardrobe as well.

It's time to put on that extra layer of seriousness, settle down, and prepare for your responsibilities.

It brings a feeling of maturation, of growth, a realization that time moves on,

And somewhere deep inside, you sense a loss . . .

It signals the end of the lackadaisical, carefree spirit that summer provides,

Yet as much as it closes the door of summer, that smell replenishes the soul.

After the summer's heat has dried up nearly all of our strength, that smell comes to lift us up and challenge our desire to live.

It has us reach down deep inside ourselves and grab hold of the energy we need to push through the fall and winter months ahead. You might say it revitalizes us.

You know, in a kind of ironic way, you might say we need that smell.

September 9, 1998

By the Water's Edge

I saw a fallen tree yesterday
by the old waterline
of the receding
lake.

It lay there on its side,
frozen and still,
like an ancient statue
felled and forgotten.

Its massive roots,
half snapped off and splintered,
had finally given way
to the eroding soil
beneath it.

It appeared the water
gradually carried away
the last of its
footing
until gravity unwaveringly
took hold, pulled and pinned
this valley oak
to where
it now
lay.

Although it had suffered . . .
To what degree,
I was not certain.

My hope was that it had been painless,
though my thoughts
conjured images
of a slow
and aching
death.

It appeared as if it had lain there,
painfully clutching,
holding on,
and slowly dying,
as it stretched, reached,
and called out
for help.
Yet no one came.

I studied it for a while longer
and wondered . . .

How long had it been down
before it finally succumbed
to the hands of time?

How long had it struggled
in the face
of its imminent death?

I wanted to have come to its aid,
to bring it back to life,
to lift it

and set it back
in its rightful place.

And deep inside,
I hurt,
knowing that I
was too late.

No one had heard its cries.
No one stopped to help.
No one cared enough.

Years of wisdom . . .
lost forever.

A pillar of strength . . .
reduced to mere wood.

One of the greatest symbols of life . . .
gone.

Guilt flooded my soul
for the failure of humanity.
Sadness overcame my heart
for the senseless loss . . .
of such significance,
such beauty.

Yet
no one listened.
No one heard.

No one,
not even the surrounding hills . . .

I . . . alone
saw a fallen tree yesterday.

July 30, 2001

Old Oak

Many a day, I passed you by
As you stood still and watched from high.
Racing from here and then to there,
We were so far and yet so near.

What made me notice you that day?
Perfectly placed, I'd have to say,
A massive presence, all alone,
Majestic beauty so unknown.

Your twisted limbs captured my gaze,
Entangled my thoughts in your maze.
I measured your girth with wide eyes,
So awestruck, I was mesmerized.

I pondered the plight of your years—
Cowboys, stagecoaches, and grazing steers,
Two children stealing their first kiss,
Lovers sharing a night of bliss.

All the changes life has shown you,
Storms you've weathered and have grown through,
The frosty winters passed away,
And months of drought from yesterday.

And who recalls an endless night,
Your shadow crawled by full moonlight

And draped across a window pane
To tell someone you're not insane?

Then year by year and inch by inch,
Come hungry hawk or tiny finch,
You welcomed all to share your shade,
Build their nests for the eggs they laid.

Such history, you don't reveal
But instead stand firm, frozen, still
To watch the mortals from up high
Obliviously pass you by.

December 30, 1998

Ode to the Old Oak

Each day,
I pass your magnificent, massive presence.
I hear you call to me,
Yet I don't know why.

I'm drawn to you like a magnet.

With so many others in view,
It is you that I seek out.
I am left unfulfilled
Until my eyes have rested upon your perfection.

I confess,
I slow down
Just to allow myself a few more precious seconds
To gaze upon and be awestricken by your grace.

One day
I want to set some time aside
To immerse myself in your story.

Your age discloses your beauty.

I've seen your great-grandchildren's great-grandchildren.
They cannot compare.

I wonder,
Am I the only one you mesmerize?

Do you have other lovers?

Your skin,
Though dry and cracked,
Conceals such fluid wisdom.
Your swollen limbs,
Though arthritically stricken,
Reveal such strength.
They reach out to me,

Beckon me closer.

You're a labyrinth
Within which I have no desire to escape.
I am hypnotized by you.
Though we have never touched,
You have touched the very heart and soul of me.

Over the years,
How many others have fallen in love with you?
How deep does your heart bleed?
As one by one, they must depart,

Are you ever lonely?

You are so strong,
Yet I'm saddened by the thought.
One day too, soon,
You may fall
By the hand of nature

Or, worse,
By someone who doesn't realize your virtue.

Or
Like all the rest,
Will I too leave you brokenhearted?

January 1, 1999

The Storm

I gazed at the rain last night
as it fell upon my bedroom window.
My eyes repeatedly followed the drops
one by one
as they raced down the pane.
Somewhere
within the darkness of the background
and the rhythmic thrumming of the drops
against the window,
I began to lose myself.

As the wind swirled and released,
I was pulled deeper into a hypnotic state.
I was drawn by the magnetic force of the storm;
it captured my strength.
My body increasingly paralyzed,
the resonance of the elements flowed through my mind,
to and fro,
back and forth,
mesmerizing my every breath.

I was swept away by a strangely comfortable numbness that
lulled my senses.
My every breath whispered
within the hollow of my skull.
For a timeless moment,
I recognized this helplessness as an omen and then
gradually surrendered to its bittersweet solitude.

A melancholy came over me
as each cell within my body
individually acknowledged
its own mortality.
Darkness stood at a distance,
beckoning and reaching out
to take my hand.

Slowly,
I extended my arm and
opened my fingers
to meet his.

Sadness filled my soul;
loss pierced my heart.
Shards of yesterday flashed before my mind's eye
as I began to fall,
spinning into an endless darkness
whose depths echoed
with a derisive laughter.

Outside, suddenly,
from the pit of its heart,
an old oak's massive limb groaned,
snapped, and came crashing into the mud.
With a marching, thunderous barrage,
the storm struck my aching heart,
demanding that I face
the turmoil, anguish, and burden
of simply existing.
My soul cried out,
my world came undone,
and I too gasped
at the loss of a limb with which to cling.

All at once,
I recognized a cruelty
within all that creates chaos and prevents calm.
My heart pounded with the speed of wild horses.
Sweat dripping,
I pressed my face against the cool glass,
frantically scouring the darkness
for some confirmation of life.

The landscape blurred
as the rain's relentless onslaught thickened
and continued to punish the window's glass
with its anger and volume.
Drowning out every surrounding sound,
it amplified the terror
that now engulfed me.
My eyes strained to focus,
but they could not discern through the shades of blackness
as it melted down the window.

The heat radiating from my face
met the cold glass
with a stinging steam.
My breathing,
shallow and rapid,
further obscured
my ability to see past the condensation
now coating the window.
I wiped madly at the cold, wet surface
in a desperate attempt to ground myself.

As I stood
clawing and staring intently,
hours seemed to pass,
though I knew
it could have been no more than a few moments.

Then something outside the window
caught my attention.
I rubbed my eyes
in an attempt to see it clearly.
I could not believe what I saw.
There, across the street,
stood the figure of a man
caught out in this dreadful storm.
Immediately,
I reached to open the window
and warn him of the danger.
But just as I unhooked the latch,
swung the window open,
and began to yell,
something stopped me.

What on earth? I thought to myself.
Though the rain still impaired my vision,
I could swear he was smiling.
With mouth agape,
I squinted,
took a closer look,
and to my growing astonishment,
he was indeed smiling!

I watched him for a few moments.
Oddly,
he seemed to be enjoying himself.
He directed his face to the sky,

stretched his arms out,
and allowed the wind and rain to blow freely
through and around him.
Then he turned his back to the elements,
repeating this peculiar behavior
over and again.

Bewildered, I watched him
for a few more moments.
Finally,
my curiosity exceeding my terror,
I felt compelled to investigate his activity
a little more closely.
I grabbed my overcoat,
hat, and galoshes
and cautiously ventured out into the storm.

From my front door,
I could see him more clearly,
though the rain continued to play tricks with his image;
he seemed to move stiltedly about,
as if in an old silent film.

Yet
with the exception of his odd behavior,
the gentleman did not appear crazy.
Instead, he seemed an older man
of apparent good health
who appeared completely unconcerned
with the storm's
destructive potential.

With much consternation,
I stepped from my front door out into the wind and rain,
for despite the hazard,

I needed to understand.
I trudged out to the sidewalk,
hunched over,
clasping my hat with one hand and holding my overcoat with the other.
The blustering wind and sharp rain
slapped me in resistance.
Momentarily questioning my own sanity
in venturing out from the safety of my home,
I nevertheless forged forward
for reasons I couldn't fully explain.

I reached a point where I stood
opposite this unusual man.
He continued lifting his chin to the storm.
Showing no fear, he laughed.
He taunted the rain.
He opened his arms
and smirked at the elements,
mocking the danger.
What foolishness, I thought.
One good bolt of lightning,
and he's finished.

Yet . . . he continued to smile,
as if
he hadn't a care in the world.
And that smile intrigued me
until I too
was compelled
to look up
into the storm's eye.

At first,
I saw violent flashes
within an endless darkness.

My earlier despair
began to flood my mind.
I found myself again
drawn into that helplessness
I so feared.

The harsh coldness began
to coat and seep into my bones.
My hands went numb.
I focused on the wetness.
I concentrated on the sound and fury
even as I held tightly to the image of my smiling comrade.
My face streaming with freezing water
and the fierce wind tearing at the roots of my past,
I stood planted
and frozen.
I tried to move
but found it
arthritically painstaking.
With much effort,
I looked at my joyful companion,
but he was too lost in his own reverie
to recognize my struggle.

Dejected,
I had all but given up
when the storm reached out
and grabbed me.
The current moved me
and knocked me off-balance.
Initially
frightened by its force,
I leaned into the storm
in an effort
to regain my ground.

Repeatedly,
it shoved
and pushed me backward,
turning me this way and that,
bullying me
as if in a schoolyard brawl.
It was then that
the shame of my fear
reached down,
awakening the depths of my anger.
Suddenly,
I refused to take any more.
Adrenaline raced through my veins.
Fire filled my eyes.
Rage became my breath.
"I choose to fight!" I shouted.

The torrent struck my face with razor-like slashes.
The wind thrust with the force of a tsunami,
but I would not relent.
The tempest's fury pulled,
tore, and clawed at me.
Its intensity punishing,
it tested my resolve.
But my determination was mountainous.

I roared into its wrath
with the ferociousness of the gods,
daring it to move me.
But it could not.
I spread my arms open wide, offering
my chest,
my will,
my life,
but it could not,

would not
diminish my spirit!

Lightning bolts lit up the night sky.
Thunder shook the earth.
The funnel of the storm
twisted and swirled
all around me,
tearing off and flinging out
fractured pieces of my heart
in every direction,
stripping me
of all the demons and terror
that once encaged me.

Finally,
its strength breathtakingly demonstrated,
with a massive roar of admiration,
the storm acknowledged my resilience
among the scattering of debris.
Yet I remained,
standing.

Still shaking
from the excess
of adrenaline and exhilaration,
I looked to see if my companion
had witnessed my victory.
My eyes searched the area where he once stood,
but he had vanished.

All at once,
I realized—
I stood in darkness,
yet though it penetrated,

it did not pierce me.
Now
the driving rains cleansed my soul.
Now
the forceful winds freed my heart.
Now
the thunder and lightning held me enthralled.

We shared in an awesome power, strength, and glory.

I leaned into the wind's powerful arms
and allowed it to take me.
For an instant,
I was weightless as it lifted me.
I was flying,
though my feet never left the ground.
I relished each and every wave of wind
as it pressed hundreds of droplets against my skin.
I found myself swimming in serenity.
The rhythm lulling my every breath and sense,
I floated along its stream
ebbing and flowing in its tide.

The wind held me, and I held it.

Mesmerized by the tranquility emanating through my body,
I smiled.
I smiled the most satisfied smile
one can imagine.
And finally,
I understood
my friend's joyful embrace of the storm.
Letting go of my fears set me free.

Back in my room,
I stood at my window,
gazed into the darkness,
and listened . . .

The wind now blew with purpose,
and all that was chaotic became collective.
The gate that clanged,
the eaves that creaked,
and the screen door that rattled
were harmonic
as each played their individual part in their celebrated symphony.
Even the fallen branch belonged just where it lay.
The night glowed with majesty.
As my fingertips slid steadily down the pane,
I awoke
as if from a dream.

Little by little,
I released myself from the storm's magnetism,
climbed back into bed,
closed my eyes,
and allowed the rain's tender lullaby
to soothe and caress my inner being.
I enjoyed the gentle temporal massage it extended
as it carried me away
in its mystical, magical reverie.

Such warmth,
I thought to myself.

Such contentment.

Such a peaceful bliss,
as I slumbered off,
comforted
by the night's
serene embrace.

March 8, 2000

Nirvana

A warm breeze gently rustles through the leaves.
On a tranquil summer's night,
I listen to nature's serenade,
Staring at a clear, dark, star-filled sky,

A peaceful place inside my mind,
Hands in my pockets, wind on my face,
A true appreciation of life,
Revealed at its own precious pace—

No worries, no stress, not even a fear
As the sweet smell of gardenias dances in my nose,
All the simple but grand treasures life yields.
So fulfilled—yet nobody knows.

Take me away, oh, gentle breeze.
Free the gravity o'er my feet.
Allow me to float
Along the currents of blissfulness
And carry me to and fro.

Let me feel your perfect harmony.
Live within and surround my entity.
Make me at home,
One with your world of blessedness.
Come embrace my sacred soul.

Like the freed feather of a dove
Falling tenderly from above,
Release me alone
To drift with ease and quiescence
Until your winds must let go.

Then lie me down softly in a bed of roses
'Til you have the strength to lift me again.

September 8, 1998

Religion

A Contemplation of Life

We ask to know the meaning of life, or
We question the reasons children die for.
If we had the answers that we strive for!
The code, you see, we couldn't decipher.

Locked in the shadows of our perception,
Our thoughts are chained in fear of deception.
Light won't enter to make that connection,
For in our mind, there is no reception.

Just like the allegory of the cave,
Our limited view has made us a slave
To the images that we solely crave.
Experience fuels the way we behave.

Until we accept this contemplation,
We're destined to live with trepidation.
Alas! May we find some consolation
Upon the theory of our creation.

March 14, 1998

Life, a Breath Away from Death

Are you afraid of death?
Can you face it like a man?
You'd best not hold your breath,
For life is just a grain of sand.

For if you fear death,
You may never face the Man,
Who gave you that first breath
And who put you on this land.

For this land is just of sand,
Which will cover you at death,
The substance that made man
A living creature by His breath.

For this sand is just a place
To roam in until death
And, to the Man life's pace,
Is just another breath.

But if you wait for death,
You'll waste your life away,
For He dictates that breath,
And until so, you will stay.

Enjoy your stay 'til death,
But don't shut out the Man,
For life without His breath
Is as fingers without a hand.

For if you leave the Man,
Who gave you that first breath,
You'll never understand
Life's not begun 'til death.

March 24, 1984

The Gift

There I was,
minding my own business,
carrying on my daily responsibilities,
nothing specific on my mind—
actually, not thinking at all,
if that's possible.
You might say I was at peace,
a condition seldom achieved.
But nonetheless,
There I was
when suddenly—
well, not even suddenly but gradually—
I was the recipient of what I believe was a gift.

Now I know everybody likes surprises
and everyone appreciates gifts,
but this was not your usual gift.
It did not come in the form of a package.
As a matter of fact, this gift would not fit in any package,
no matter how large or small.
This gift came in the form of a pleasing sound.

At first, I was unaware of the gift,
but as I said, it gradually entered my ears.
The next thing I knew, a feeling came unto me,
like nothing I had known before.
My soul had been awakened.

The melody wrapped itself around my soul
and then set out in all directions until the harmony reached the end of
my extremities.
A humming, a buzzing, took over my entire being,
while the rhythm matched my heartbeat, beat for beat.

Finally, I became conscious of this euphoria flowing through me.
I relished it. I wanted it to go on forever. I didn't want this feeling to
ever escape me.
I bathed in it 'til the music ended. And for a period after, I treasured it.
I didn't know the song. I had never heard it before; nor have I since.
I didn't know the author. And no, I didn't see any angels.
I can't say I even thought of them at the time.
You know, I didn't even consider it a religious experience—then.

But as I sit before this page with the memory of that event,
I can't help but think that someone accidentally broke off a piece of
heaven
and that I was fortunate enough to be standing where it landed.

March 15, 1998

A Step in Time

Come with me, those who dare,
To the last breath of your life.
Let's take a step through the veil
And see what we may find.
Are you afraid you'll never be
allowed to go back home?
That's just the chance you'll have to take
To taste the unknown!

Just close your eyes and go to sleep.
You may never know you left.
Oh, don't be frightened by the thought
You've ended life by theft.
I only propose this little trip
So that we can take a peek.
There's so much more to learn about.
Turn back if you're too weak!

Will we discover a whole new world
Or nothing new at all?
Perhaps we really haven't gone;
It's just time that has been stalled.
Look ahead or just behind.
You'll see what you've become.
But just don't try to change it.
It's already done!

Welcome to the other side.
It's true; there's no way back.
That image of yourself you see
Is on another track.
Soon enough, you'll forget about
The other side of time.
And just when you're adjusted,
We'll make another climb!

August 6, 1998

Heaven

A transparent stairway through the clouds,
A choir of angels singing of love—
A subtle breeze fills the air.
The scenario is a state of quiescence.
The spirits are at peace and harmony.
All the colors are of pastel.
The sense and creation of all of nature,
The experience of everlasting life,
No pain,
No guilt,
No jealousy,
To release and drift away—
The dream of all wonderful dreams.
But how can it seem so real?
For it's only the imagination of a lonely man
Passed on throughout the centuries.

February 18, 1986

A Question to Believers

A question to believers:
In which pot shall I pay
To save my soul from the devil's hold
And live another day?
Should I give to you who ask
To divide my worth by ten
Or you who'll pass a basket
And allow my heart to spend?
Then there are some who'll gladly ask
To take a minute of my time
Until I kindly excuse myself
And try to sort my mind.
And yet there are those who'll say
The others are all wrong—
"Just look at this and read that.
We want you to belong."
When finally, I collect my thoughts,
I confess, I laugh a bit.
So similar are their puzzle pieces,
Yet so afraid are they to admit.
So I ask to you believers:
Why do you want my pay?
Is it to save my precious soul
From the wolves out for the prey?

July 27, 1998

Paths

Some paths lead down winding roads
Whose destinations are a mystery.
Who knows where their end erodes
Or what belies within their history?

Yet some are direct and to the point,
Mocking the challenge in one's choice,
Though it's only us who can anoint
Upon the hark of our heart's voice.

Some paths are sought out of a yearning
As independence seeks insight
Until the time we end up returning
To the ideals we'd wished to fight.

Some paths are freedom in and of themselves,
And direction is of no great concern.
Yet time will lead us to ourselves
When we have nowhere to turn.

And there are paths of trial and error
Presenting success and failure alike,
Calling within us to overcome the terror
Upon the cliffs of experience we hike.

Yet some are marked with ample warnings,
Claiming risk and future cost,

But it's not 'til our hearts are mourning
That we realize what's lost.

And I hear of one, intense with light,
From the horizon to the sky,
We all alone must face despite
The days and years gone by.

Still, there are new paths ever burning
Within the dreamer's night,
And all paths lead to greater learning,
Though we choose wrong or right.

March 29, 2001

Christmas

Christmas is that time of year
When special memories fill the air.
The streets are decorated with colorful lights,
While chimneys are puffing into cold winter nights.
The children are happy; it's this time of year
As they wait for the man with the long white beard.
Faces are glowing, and love is all around.
Joy is overflowing as the bells begin to sound.
Yes, it's Christmastime once again
When strangers become the best of friends.

December 19, 1985

Love

Love

I've thought long and hard about this word and the array of meanings we attribute to it. At times, I'm left without a way to fully describe it. It encompasses such a variety and breadth of definitions that often leaves me dumbfounded. Yet here I am, attempting to put into words what I believe captures the essence of it. Though I fear deep down that I will not do such a magnificent word justice, I persist in the endeavor.

It is so often that I hear it used with what seems to me such trivialness that I question the veracity of our desire to truly comprehend the magnitude of its meaning and influence. Individually and as a global collective, we rarely take the time to immerse ourselves in its purest form. I proffer we'd be so much more different, better for the impact that it would have on us all, if we did. Yet if we did, why does it seem so difficult for one to imagine a world where conflict born out of fear does not exist?

Remove all the defense mechanisms, all the excuses, and all you have left is fear. For fear is at the root of all that prevents love. Only once fear is removed is there left a heart open to acceptance, ready to be filled with love. For genuine love and fear cannot exist simultaneously.

It is unfortunate that today's perceived definition is so fragile. Cheapening the true definition only adds to the fear and causes many to avoid love at all costs. How many hearts have been broken by our misperception and misrepresentation of love?

I believe that *love* is the most commanding word in the English language, the most powerful emotion known to man. I believe it is the seed from which all things become possible, and it brings with it the promise of all great things to come. With love in one's heart, the sun burns warmly, the winds blow gently, and the rain cleanses away all that challenges the truth. It is the one emotion that brings walls of difference crumbling down and lifts chins of dejection toward the sky. It would seem then that such a word having such significance would warrant more discreet application.

It guarantees success where all else leave room for failure. It breeds only itself yet is everything that one could hope for in and of itself. When one gives love to another, both are purified in its glory. When one refrains from the sharing of love, that one is left without the true meaning and understanding of love.

Love is more than a feeling and more than an experience. It is not bound by time, space, or any one dimension. Love is unconditional. It is more transparent than air yet possesses more substance than any matter. Real love expands infinitely, piercing and permeating all it touches.

Love is the ability to accept differences, have compassion for and comfort those whose circumstances have left them without hope. Love is tender, bright, and beaming with a passion that overflows the body's ability to contain it. Love nurtures all that is good and right with a discerning, guiding, and tempered hand. Love knows not of jealousy, greed, possessiveness, or selfishness. Rather, it understands, shares, frees, and is selfless.

Love is being your own best friend and sharing that with the world. For a moment, imagine love as a way of life.

A Change for the Better

(Change an Inevitability)

My life is changing,
Moving into the fast lane.
My ideas are changing
As I venture a new plain.
My love is changing for you
But only for the better.
I must change,
For it is part of maturity.
You will change,
For you are in need of security.
My love will change for you
But only for the better.
I will change
'Til I find my fraternity.
For change will change
Forever through eternity.
And my love will change for you
But only for the better.

April 1, 1984

Beauty

Beauty is something that's everlasting,
With all the elegance of a dove.
Beauty is something that's ever surpassing
All the clouds high above.

Beauty is something that's sweet and innocent,
Like the petals of a rose.
Beauty is something that, when sensed,
Will fill the heart and tickle the nose.

Beauty is something that's hard to find,
Even if searched for near and far.
Beauty is something that's warm and kind
And as peaceful as a floating star.

July 11, 1985

Body of Wine

February 24, 1999

Her hair
Is sculpted
And shiny,

Her eyes
Glowing
And
Seductive.

When she
Smiles, joy
Fills the air.

Her neckline
Proffers such

Curves of elegance.

Her throat swallows the
Passion that I've thirsted for.
When she breathes, I am there.

She has such sensuous shoulders.

She has smooth, gentle hands; when
She touches me, I'll know she cares.

Her essence is sweet and romantic,
Her dress conservative and classy.

When she's near me, I feel no fear.

Her legs are long and silky, her walk

Of the utmost poise and confidence.

When
She leaves me, then begin the tears.

Shooting Stars

They ignited like flame and a fuse, exploding like fireworks with showering brilliance and excitement. But as with fireworks, the beautiful glow gave way to the remnants of smoke and the heavy blackness of the midnight sky.

The collision was fast. It came upon their hearts and spun with the speed of tornadoes. They grabbed for each other and hung on for the ride of their lives. But as with tornadoes, what once was awesome and fascinating turned into a whirlwind of chaos and confusion.

The fever was reckless. Throwing caution to the wind, they raced without direction toward the unknown. But as with races, while there are winners and losers, there are also some who never reach the end.

The fury was over, ending somewhere in the night on some unfamiliar road leading to nowhere.

Yet for one fleeting moment, their radiance lit up the sky.

April 10, 1999

Beyond an Appetite

The world outside is melting
as the molecules begin to dance.
Tonight the animal sleeps,
as he has for many moons.
Hibernation has been so restful,
but the season is coming to an end.
Deep in the pit of his loins,
a painful yearning begins to awake.
Instinct is aroused
as his aching glands salivate.
Driven by a burning thirst,
he soon must abandon his cave,
Surrender to an insatiable hunger
that compels his very being.
Further forbearance
would devour any chance of survival.
He breaks free
from the solace of his protection.
He stands erect
with heightened sensitivity and awareness.
His bodily secretions
come alive to reach their zenith.
He plunges in
and tears the flesh from his prey.
The aroma fills his nostrils

as the flavor drips from his chin.
The famine is conquered
as he releases a primal roar.

April 2, 1998

Love Lives

April 9, 1999

Then without warning, air seems to fill his lungs, and as it pushes upward through his nostrils, breaking the seal of his lips, it forces his face to quiver with such overflowing joy and happiness that he knows at that moment that love lives.

They are alone as one, together, yet surrounded by the birds that sing, the dogs that bark, the sound of the people and cars that pass. They share a glowing gaze into each other's eyes that stills the winds of time and simultaneously sees into the future, promising all that is and all that will be.

Her caring hand, gentle as a lullaby, strokes with its sensitive fingers the inside of his palm, reassuring an everlasting bond and eternal commitment as strong as the length of time.

There are flowers in bloom emitting fragrances of freshness and painting rainbows of colors that only a new spring can offer under the guise of hope.

A garden flourishing with trees, possessing the beauty of all the greens on the artist's palette, brings forth the rebirth and growth of a love once dormant. And now protected by the canopy from the subtle winds of change that once carried the uncertainty of tomorrow, they cling tightly to each other.

Two hearts locked in a common beat pump adoration to the very ends of their beings, sending vibrating sensations that permeate through and beyond them.

There is music, which only they can hear. It is soft, it is sweet, and it is of violins yet to be scored, crying and pleading their love.

They embrace, acknowledging all they have shared as their tears join the brook and flow under the bridge of yesterday.

In an atmosphere that has cleared, the ranges of distant mountains meet in the valley and share such a depth and closeness that they truly are one, while the bluest of skies hangs virgin-white fluffs that float on by in their own space of peace and serenity.

An inner warmth grows inside, with the intimacy of flames intertwined in a romantic slow dance coveting every ebb and flow. Then fanning outward like the ocean's tide, which comes to blanket the shore with its soothing caress, it retreats and permits the granules of sand to exhale a sigh of relief.

Not a word to be spoken as thoughts ride on the waves of tender emotions . . .

They are one, one unto themselves, one with God's creatures, and one with all of nature, reunited.

Understanding of Love

They say love will lead to happiness.
They say heaven is high above.
I say, my love, I only know loneliness.
I say they don't understand love.

I've had the love I once nurtured so tenderly.
I've lost that love I once thought was mine.
I'll give again my love so willing but carefully.
I'll never quit on my love until I find.

They say love will lead to happiness.
They say heaven is high above.
I say, my love, I only know patience.
I say they may understand love.

I've found the love I will nurture so tenderly.
I'll hold it close, for it is mine.
I'll share my love so willingly and freely.
I'll always be true to the love that I find.

They say love will lead to happiness.
They say heaven is high above.
I say, my love, I only know truthfulness.
I say I now understand love.

January 15, 1986

Heartbreak

What heart cries silent tears at night
When emptiness overwhelms it?
How dost heartache turn off love's light,
Which so intensely once was lit?

What nights are made of sleepless thoughts
And hollow eyes that can't be fed?
What days are born for wrenching knots
That draw me curled upon my bed?

What sorrow reigns this wounded soul
And besieges my every breath?
Why must this grief take full control
When love's fire's been put to death?

Such passions fade beyond true love
As despondence overcomes me,
And heaven's torch crumbles above,
While dark thoughts plague my sanity.

How long must I endure this pain
Of brokenhearted misery?
How would you feel to find me slain,
Knowing it was your injury?

Why must this knife refuse to cease
The madness that penetrates me?

Is it too late to find some peace?

My beloved, I shall free thee.

Now drop by drop,
My heart shall bleed
A pure satin-red agony.

Where is my god?

Must I too plead?

Ah! The numbness

Overtakes

Me.

January 30, 1999

Divorce

The sharpest knife I ever threw pierced a hole through time.

November 6, 1998

❧

Gemini

Burnt umber ladled with the sun's golden glare,
Streams, twists, and curls into long auburn hair,

Distinct forest green peppered with canary and black,
Eyes of the Nile bringing Mark Antony back,

Strawberry cream with a powdered sugar trace,
Soft as a rose petal caressing your face,

Corvette red—lacquered, polished, and shined—
A mysterious smile hides behind,

Mint chiffon against the midnight blue,
Crashing waves under a moonlit hue,

The scent of coconut, a bronze embrace,
A fiery passion time can't erase

Until . . .

Battleship grey conquers sky-blue dreams,
Changing golden to yellow and off-color creams.

The forest is jaded with envy and spite,
Pupils that pierce a black onyx night,

Sweetness that spoils into death's pale shade,
Cold as blue cobalt, sharp as a blade,

Satin-red flows thicker than blood,
Suppressing rage, dark as the bayou's mud,

Salmon to sienna, leather and suede,
Losing the luster as passion starts to fade,

Deserted, marooned, left all alone,
Disposed of, depleted, skeleton bone.

May 12, 2000

Where There Is Pain

Dark and light set in motion,
Chaotic chemistry has no notion.
So bright a star could burn so hot.
Upon his map is merely a dot.

Relativity determined its fate,
Discounted by those too busy to wait.
Its glimmer and sparkle begin to fade,
Redirected by matter, the price it paid.

A shimmering tail streams from the remains.
Dark replaces light where there is pain—

Tempered breaths of the placid ocean,
Thunder and lightning filled with commotion,
The morning dew of love once forgot,
Saline reminders of love for naught.

A lunar pulse governed its gate,
Elided by hearts regardless of state.
Its flame and devotion will dissipate,
Annulled by white angels of hate.

Sparked solely by passion of another name,
Dark replaces light where there is pain.

Seedlings awakened for their promotion,
Soil trampled by oblivious emotion,

Rainbows promise of a golden pot.
Grass grew greener in a barren spot.

Fertility reigns to procreate,
Displaced by mirages of younger days.
Oak trees crack, frozen and gray,
Jaded milkweeds that asphyxiate.

Bitter sweetness stems from the cane.
Dark replaces light where there is pain.

January 20, 1997

Him

I see him growing.
I recognize his eyes.
I know his dreams.
I feel his pain.

His heart loves the world.
His feelings, he can't yet express.
He is quietly thinking.

His will knows determination.
He longs for acceptance.
He is still a child.

He plays with intensity.
He fights with rage.
He cares more than he shows.

He is not guarded.
He laughs freely.
He hates to cry.
He tries to be strong.

He is the middle child.
He sacrifices.
He knows tenderness.
He asks for nothing.

He is brave and scared.
He is me all over.
He is my son.
He makes me proud.

He means the world.

April 14, 1999

My Final Blossom

You of she and me,
You of me and she,

You of he and she,
You of she and he,

You of complex roots,
Dividing and splintering,

You of them and they,
You of all,

You . . .

A glorious fruit
Of all that is good and sweet,

You . . . a perfect peach

You . . .

My final blossom

February 11, 2002

My Final Blossom II

Baby's breath with rose petal lips
Grafted from an oak and a daisy,
A miniature carnation of pink and white,
A wild flower growing like crazy,
Light as a lily, delicate as the dew
On the dawn's early daffodil bud—
The trumpets will blow and the golden horns cry
As you break through the humus and mud.
A dozen of iris, a tad of green,
Waking to a morning of glory,
A beautiful bouquet befitting a queen
Mums the word of your babbling story.
Fresh as the freesia, pure as the poppy,
A posy of violet and red,
A sweet buttercup, an orange azalea,
An arrangement from toe to head,
A pretty little pansy, a precious petunia,
At peace in your bed come night,
A glamorous gladiola, an oil-painted orchid
Of all that is perfect and right—
Tulips cannot speak of the stars in your eyes.
Crocus can't call you awesome.
Yet from an old oak to a bird of paradise,
I'm in love with my final blossom.

February 12, 2002

Friendship

Few gifts known to man can match that of friendship. It is the closest relative to love, providing the unconditional acceptance we all, as social beings, yearn for.

Friendship realizes the imperfection of the human being while striving for the greatest effort at being human. It is patient, and it is honest. It is loyal and forgiving.

Friendship listens without judgment, gives without taking, and understands without explanation.

Friendship shares in more than just your successes and failures; it shares in your everyday experiences of life with an empathy that parallels that of an angel's heart.

Friendship is selfless, setting aside its immediate interests for the needs of another.

Friendship is mutual. It allows for each to be strong and each to feel weak.

Friendship is admiration, a willingness to recognize the uniqueness and gifts of another.

Friendship is timeless. It resumes where it left off after the interruptions of life have temporarily subsided.

It's one of the most gratifying experiences known to humanity where our appetite is satisfied with few.

Friendship loves.

December 29, 1999

Just a Bit Benign

It was Sunday noon at the baseball park.
I found my seat next to my near friend Clark.

I asked how was his? He asked how was mine?
Same ol' greetings, and everything was fine,
Nothing really deep, just a bit benign.

We stood with the crowd, and the anthem played.
We removed our caps o'er the field of jade.

When the hotdogs came, we drank lemonade
'Til the sunlight's arc cast us in the shade.

I asked how was his? He asked how was mine?
Same ol' exchange, and everything was fine,
Nothing really deep, just a bit benign.

It was Sunday eve at the baseball park
As I tipped my cap to my near friend Clark.

January 27, 1999

Loss

Death's Light

Death is life's greatest recognition.

January 30, 1999

～⚘～

Accepting Death

A scream to pierce dark deaf skies
While smirking gods fold their arms,
Running without direction,
Apathetic to the consequence
To pummel the ocean's sandy beach
'Til the spray cuffs through the exhaustion—

Question on knees the knowing stars.
Wide eyes hope a light will shine.
Recognize a familiar path
Liberated from this labyrinth.
Arthritic limbs flow together
As the tide smooths out the ripples.

At long last, a glimmering tear
Falls peacefully into the night,
Stepping stones in life's garden
Where yellow ribbon daffodils grow.
The crying seagull heads for home
As the ball of fire slowly subsides.

October 1, 1995

Behind the Glass Door

(Two Months)

Are you smiling down at me
With those eyes that owned compassion?
Do you reach out for me
With your arms of warm embrace?
I wonder if you try to touch me
With your caress while I'm asleep.
Can your thoughts still guide me
Through so much I wish to know?

January 23, 1998

Seasons Pass

(Three Months)

Diminishing memories of a pain so sweet,
Ambiguous thoughts of guilt and peace,

Shards of recollection without warning—
Time stops in a moment of mourning.

Yesterday's heartache begins to mend,
Desires to cling on until the end.

Obscurity defines the road ahead.
Gravity relinquishes feet of lead.

Images recalled when seasons pass.
Melancholy empties its glass.

February 27, 1998

My Grandmother's Daughter

A child of hers, a mother of mine,
To each a lifetime's work,
A parent's pride, a child's stride,
Removed by nature's quirk—

A mother's pain can't be compared
To the tragedies of life.
A child's heart will soon be spared
As time is on its side.

Yesterday's heartache begins to heal
For those who do not bear,
Yet such memories are still so real
Through the eyes of wisdom's years.

Days go by, and a child grows.
Scarce memories remain
Until the circle has been exposed.
Now the parent understands such pain.

Nothing but the best for the mother's child,
A wall of marble to cry upon—
She's the only one left after a while.
She'll be the last one gone.

Only the best for this mother's child,
A world of acceptance to live within—

She'll be the face when I smile
And share her love again.

A child of hers, a mother of mine,
To each a lifetime's gift,
A child's sun, a parent's shine,
To whom our hearts, we lift.

November 18, 1998

Mama, You're Home

And so you've succumbed to the natural order
of men leaving your remaining
offspring here to defend what you had
placed at the top of all others, a glorious
belief sought only by mothers.

Love for family demonstrated in each
action, your example reverberates in
whole and in fraction within and
throughout every seed and season 'til what
some see as illogic is overtaken by reason.

The wall of marble that once pulled you in
like a magnet now holds you captive in an
air that lies stagnant, for those who
frequent and mourn on their own may
never comprehend how much you are home.

In a cruel test of your faith time and again,
you returned to this wall to lay to rest your
children. Not once or twice would you
weep before the fine marble, but an
agonizing thrice should you have to endure
as your children's candles went dark far before yours.

Their hopes and dreams and seeds of their own
became simply part of the burden and load
you carried to keep the promise you made
when you tucked them in tightly in the bed where they lay.

Now given the full understanding of such,
it isn't a stretch to comprehend as much
As the love of a mother to long to be near
the most preciously held, the earnestly dear.

So if you should pass the wall, don't be mistaking
her name as one of the sadly forsaken.
She rests quite peacefully knowing the climb was steep
and long but the reward sublime,
where at the end, she is close as the heart may keep
a mother and child at rest, at sleep.

June 1, 2018

By Any Other Name

(My Mother's Garden)

How dare these words must I repeat
By any other name would smell as sweet
By any other name would smell as sweet

By any other name
By any other name
That's such a shame
By any other name
What a cruel game
By any other name

I passed the place where she'd retreat
The echoes in my mind are incomplete
By any other name should smell as sweet
By any other name should smell as sweet

By any other name
By any other name
What a cruel game
By any other name

She'd sensually inhale their treat
Exclaim in the midst of the summer's heat
By any other name would smell as sweet
By any other name would smell as sweet

By any other name
By any other name

Her velvet touch met with defeat
That splendorous essence once so discreet
By any other name can't smell as sweet
By any other name can't smell as sweet
What a cruel game
By any other name

Why must these words I dare repeat
By any other name would smell as sweet
By any other name would smell as sweet

It's such a shame
By any other name won't smell as sweet

What a cruel game
What a cruel game
By any other name
By any other name

September 27, 1999

And You

My eyes see darkness and light,
Reflections of rainbows,
Shades of gray,
And you.
My nose breathes deep and full
Confections of flowers,
Aromas in the air,
And you.
My ears hear silence and sound,
Harmony of music,
A clock's tick,
And you.
My fingers feel coldness and heat,
Gradations of textures,
A pin's prick,
And you.
My lips taste bitterness and sweet,
Liquids that quench,
A lover's kiss,
And you.
And you?

July 22, 1998

Out of Nowhere

(January 2, 2001: 12:39 p.m.)

It was out of nowhere on the above date and time.
I almost grabbed the phone 'cause you crossed my mind.
I thought I'd call just to chew on your ear,
For your voice was really all I wanted to hear.

Then I stopped myself as I leaned toward the phone
And realized you wouldn't be home,
For you left me more than three years ago
To some faraway place I do not know.

For a moment, that long-ago melancholy returned,
Along with the memory of a heart that yearned,
And anger of your absence ignited and burned
'Til I smothered its flame with all that I've learned.

Still perplexed, I paused and then walked slowly away,
Pondered the reasons of why now and today,
Though I held on to the thought for only a while,
Told myself, "I'm just crazy" and started to smile.

On a more serious note, I wanted to know
Yet knew that such questions ebb and flow.

But still,

Ain't it strange that what used to be there
Can suddenly arise out of nowhere?

January 2, 2001

The Dream

I long for the day
When I can see your smile
And your eyes can connect with mine.
You don't have to speak
A word all the while.
Your expression will tell me you're fine.

In your eyes,
The world was a happy place.
In your presence, I felt so much love.
I yearn for the time
When we'll stand face-to-face,
Yet the clock can't tick fast enough.

So I learn
To live without you here
And remember all that you taught.
Still, I wonder when
That day will finally appear
When I'll reach the dream that I've sought.

August 5, 1998

Hope

The leaves of autumn have left their branches
Exposed to the winter cold,
Like the love that once sheltered me
From the years of growing old.

The dark clouds filled with moisture
Roll in to heavy my load,
Like the hues of gray and black
That fall upon this lonely road.

The welcomed thunder and lightning
Release an angry tone,
Snapping, cracking, and roaring
As my heart begins to moan.

Then . . .

The rhythm of the wind and rain
Massage the window's glass
Like the touch that once caressed me
To peaceful dreams, alas.

The morning's light is blinding
As it confirms another day,
Scattered thoughts strewn about a yard,
The night before affray'd.

The scent of nature in the air
Refreshes a peaceful calm,
Like the rainbows in the distance
Promised to sing a psalm.

February 1, 1998

Dust

Eventually, we all settle.

February 23, 1999

Wounded

Motherhood at Youth

She was young and wild and running with her friends,
But the time had come for that all to end.

She met someone who made her feel good.
He made her do things she never thought she would.

They were loving and living, playing husband and wife.
She was ignoring her family, her friends, and her life.

Then one day it happened, and the fun was over.
She found that what she needed was a friend to hold her.

The "father to be" said he was going to the store.
Little did she know she would see him no more.

She couldn't go back to her family, her friends,
Whom she had ignored, said she'd never depend.

Now she's alone, feeling betrayed, lost, and scared.
She wishes there were someone, someone who cared.

She remembers her friends and the fun that they had,
Doings things just for kicks, being good, being bad.

She thinks of her family, upon whom she would not depend.
She curls up on the bench and begins to descend,

Holding herself. Her future feels bleak.
If you look real close, you'll see the tears on her cheek.

She was young and wild and running with her friends,
But the time has come for that all to end.

May 2, 1984

Tears

A scared child hiding in a perilous world,

A lonely child crying herself to sleep,

A confused child contemplating suicide,

An abused child—why must she have to survive?

February 9, 1986

She

She doesn't cry for the nutrients that would sustain her.
How could she? She has a different craving.

She doesn't have a bond with the mother who bore her.
How could she? She was torn away so quickly.

She doesn't comprehend the lessons they teach her.
How could she? She suffers from ADD.

She doesn't question the world that controls her.
How could she? She has low self-esteem.

She doesn't confront the men who abuse her.
How could she? She is still a child.

She doesn't hear the angels who call unto her.
How could she over her silent screams?

She doesn't know what's growing inside her.
How could she? She is barely thirteen.

She doesn't understand the pain that plagues her.
How could she when the scar runs so deep?

She doesn't dream. She doesn't wonder.
She doesn't even hope.

She doesn't want to live in this world that surrounds her.

How could she?

Why should she?

January 5, 2000

"Forgive Me," "I'm Sorry," "I Didn't Mean To"

Intimidated, scared, and confused—
It was the first day of high school.

The hallways were suffocating
As he retrieved her fallen books

"Forgive me, "I'm sorry," "I didn't mean to,"
And she accepted his apology.
They strode to class together—
Room 22, subject psychology.

Obsessive, insecure, and low self-esteem—
The teacher taught them well.
Together, they fit perfectly,
But the pages did not reveal

Rage, anger, and inhibitions,
All exposed by alcohol,
A side of him she never knew,
Like the names that she was called.

"Forgive me," "I'm sorry," "I didn't mean to,"
And she accepted his apology.
He seemed sincere and swore
They were words he'd never repeat.

Steadily, gradually, and reluctantly,
She surrendered her control.
Just like her grandmother's daughter,
She felt she was born to fulfill a role.

Their hopes, promises, and love
Grew like an infectious disease.
Her freedom of expression
Was her first right to cease.

"Forgive me," "I'm sorry," "I didn't mean to,"
And she accepted his apology,
This time a bit reluctantly,
But the diamond had a certain ring.

The days, months, and years
Held secrets to be kept
As the monster in her nightmares
Lay beside her when she slept.

Purple, black, and blue,
The colors she came to despise,
Could not be camouflaged;
Nor the swelling around her eyes.

"Forgive me," "I'm sorry," "I didn't mean to,"
And he accepted her apology.
If only she'd try harder,
He wouldn't have to be so mean.

The pain, hurt, and agony
Of allowing it to continue
Grew worse than any punch or kick
That she could ever construe.

Ups, downs, ins, and outs—
She couldn't keep up with the pace.
She'd find the strength and courage
With the help of God's grace.

"Forgive me," "I'm sorry," "I didn't mean to,"
The words with forgotten meaning,
Echoed in her beaten head
Long after she said, "I'm leaving."

October 8, 1995

House of Pain

December 3, 1998

As I turn the worn key, the heavy latch unlocks the door just as it has thousands of times before. Yet this time, it echoes through the empty cell where rebellious, surly youth once existed. The air that once carried the scent of teenage sweat and tension now lies stale and dormant. Years' worth of carvings, profanity still remain on the solid wooden doors. Etchings in the metal frames of the bunks bolted to the walls reveal the names of the now lonely, stagnant minds left there to repent their sins.

I can't help but recall the voices, the fear, and the rage that consumed every square inch of this place—such brave and angry young men with enough defiance to take on the world by themselves.

Sadly, these children belonged to someone, sometime, yet somehow they became doomed, damned, and condemned by a society that wanted no part of them and the choices they'd made. I can still hear the staff trying to shape and save these threadbare souls, preaching hope and issuing edicts that are rarely heard. And still, there are those who would be content with closing them behind these heavy doors with an easy turn of the key.

Fights would break out, and a housing area would explode. Kids would be restrained, their arms and wills bent behind their backs, put in a dark isolation room where the walls of time engulfed the strongest of minds. There were tears and screams, bitter laughter and unanswered prayers.

The cold concrete and cinderblock became home for many. They'd return time after time, some with false smirks and others with genuine frowns. Mom and Dad couldn't manage them, though they were rare if they had both. They were victims of alcoholism, drug addiction, abuse, or just plain neglect. This place held more secrets, lies, and broken dreams than one could ever imagine. Life was expendable. Many tied their sheets and contemplated death. Very few followed through successfully.

Though silence now befalls these walls, I still hear the ghosts of youth long gone kick these doors and yell obscenities through their windows. As for me, I'll leave my key hanging here in this lock to free the last of the forgotten spirits, turn away and pray the demolition crew soon levels this house of pain.

House of Pain

(Part 2)
October 11, 2002

The demolition crew arrived today. Yet as I stood outside the cyclone fencing, solemnly staring at the defenseless structure, this day that I had waited so long for suddenly seemed to arrive too soon.

Although it had been years since the evacuation and I thought I had exorcised all the demons, my mind raced with a myriad of emotions all swirling and colliding into one another . . . Did they know what they were about to destroy? Had they given any thought to the significance of this structure or its past occupants? Couldn't they see the writings, the small rooms, the cold history, the good intentions? Didn't they care? Want to understand? Could they ever?

Bewildered, I stood in my personal hell and watched this surreal scene as the workers planned their attack underneath the break of dawn and the idling of their oversized Tonka toys. The cool air, lightly scented with the smell of diesel fuel, carried a much heavier and darker omen as the mammoth machines sat like ravenous prehistoric dinosaurs panting, salivating, and impatiently waiting to pounce on and devour their helpless prey.

As the workers returned to their posts and revved up their engines, the landscape seemed to move in slow motion. The roar of the beasts was deafening and derisive as it immediately broke and consumed the morning's tranquility. As the dust kicked up, it bellowed and hung in the air like a magician's smoke in the midst of a disappearing trick. And just as they moved in for the kill, I felt a sudden urge to yell to the

119

workers and tell them to stop, hold off . . . wait for just one moment longer. But why and for what, I had no idea.

The first of many strikes landed with a thunderous blow. The ground beneath my feet shook as the vibration traveled throughout my body and awoke a real fear of the brutality and actual destructive powers of such a collision. As bits and pieces flung out and fell to the ground, somewhere in the midst of my numbness, I hurt. And although I could not discern from where the pain emanated, I felt ill. All I could think of was the innocuous innocence of the building. It did not ask for its role; nor did it deserve this fate. No one did. And yet with each repeated blow, somewhere within the hollows of the tunnel from which I now stood, I heard the cries of the past, I saw the faces of the children, and I cursed the inequities of our society.

Paralyzed still, I watched. I watched as the first wall came crumbling down. I watched as the machines relentlessly punished its pillars. I watched as the stubborn rebar clung firmly to its blocks. I watched as the machines pulled, tore, and twisted it until it finally succumbed to the torture and hung lifeless and mangled among the rubble. I watched but could do nothing to save it.

Still half lost in the horrifying experience of the destruction and half caught up in the emotions of yesteryear, I slowly retreated.

Hours later, as I sat at my desk, I contemplated the strange irony of the building and its once threadbare occupants, and I half-smiled inside as I rationalized their somewhat awkward symbiotic relationship: both victims of circumstance, both in need of the other, and both obstinate 'til the end.

Day after day, the workers returned. Day after day, I'd stop to take a moment's look but found the view less and less palatable and soon beyond recognition.

Later, the sounds became muffled until one day they were gone—but only from my ears.

Miscellaneous
Perspectives/
Philosophies

Fall of Morality

Since when did we have any choice
To speak our minds via our voice?
A firm hand spoke the only truth.
Where are the obedient youth?

'Twas once when our guidance was sure
And parents would preach only pure,
Would protect every eye and ear
From the evils frightfully near.

'Twas then when we learned to behave
And deny the wrongs that enslave,
When conscience was more than a thought
And honesty fervently sought.

'Twas once when our leaders stood tall.
Principles were not protocol.
They believed without use of sight
In the laws they knew were right.

But today such values are tossed.
Outside, many people are lost.
Direction has ceased to exist
As the pulpits no longer persist.

The ethics we used to embrace
With probity, honor, and grace,

We've discarded without just cause,
Resulting in serious flaws.

Earnestly must we own the blame
For the ills that cause us such shame.
There's just fear we'll never return
To a life of righteous concern.

January 20, 1999

Measure of a Man

Is it in time that some measure our lives?
Is all that we were, is all that survives?

Yet the "day by day" may never be known.
The secrets we hold when we're all alone,
We bury beneath a garden of stone.

It is not time that determines our drives,
A genuine picture of our true lives.
To this must we all consider alone
A bloody trail that leads us to the zone.

But without the fantasies man contrives
Within his head, often evil connives,
A scar cut deep into all of our lives.

What's in the heart should we only condone,
For when he expires, that's all he can own.

February 9, 1998

Only to Survive

(Fear of Failure)

Don't praise me for the things I do,
For I am trying only to survive.

Don't raise me above my comrades,
For I am fighting only to survive.

Your support has been well taken,
For I am struggling only to survive.

But I can sense the grasping claws of failure.
I run only to survive.

March 30, 1986

Optimists vs. Pessimists

June 2001

Given the choice of optimism or pessimism, I can see how one could easily gravitate toward the former. Optimists are positive and shine light on the darkest of circumstances. When all else seems doomed, the optimist offers hope and gives one something to believe in. The often and overused "glass half full" saying quickly comes to mind when one thinks of the optimist. The optimist appears more cheerful and smiles more frequently. Who wouldn't want to be affiliated with such joy and happiness?

Yet it is the pessimist who would question such exuberance. Why should one always have the tendency to be looking at things through such rose-tinted glasses? The world isn't perfect. There is and always has been sorrow and tragedy in the world. And there will continue to be. Why should one assume things are going to change? Hope is simply a matter of luck. The pessimist believes he views the world through eyes of realism. Pessimists don't smile nearly as much and often hide behind eyes of suspicion.

Then given the option, why is it that most people tend to prefer optimists to pessimists? Is it as simple as they are better company? I do not believe so entirely. It is my belief that most people have experienced their share of positive and negative outcomes in their lives. And it is in this area that I believe the optimists have experienced greater favorable outcomes than the pessimists. The question is then is this greater favorable outcome a matter of luck or attributed to some other influence?

Let's focus on the word *hope*. What is hope? Defined, it means to wish for something with the expectation of its fulfillment, to look forward to with confidence or expectation—trust.

When one hopes, does one who is the optimist place a greater possibility of achieving their outcome versus one who is a pessimist?

Fulfillment, expectation, confidence, and *trust*—these are all words that lend themselves to positive thinking. When one is fulfilled, one is satisfied. When one has expectation, one has promise and direction. When one is confident, one is self-assured. And when one has the ability to trust, one has security.

It is my belief that the optimist places much more emphasis in this frame of mind than does the pessimist. Optimists revel more in their fulfillment, expect favorable results, utilize more confidence, and trust that all will end well.

I believe the pessimist has difficulty in embracing these terms based upon his prior experiences. Fulfillment is short-lived as they expect that worse things are to come, thereby stifling their confidence and placing them on unsure footing. Trust is a liability, and caution is where security lies.

And it is here where I believe the scales of equality and justness begin to tilt in favor of the optimist.

For every act that the optimist is rewarded for, he is reinforced that he is making the correct decision/assumption. The optimist takes pride in his accomplishment and looks forward to the next challenge. For every act wherein he does not receive his desired outcome, he looks for reasons to improve or correct his actions to obtain his desired outcome, thereby putting forth that much more effort than does the pessimist on endeavors, which are thwarted with obstacles.

In contrast, when the pessimist receives his desired outcome, he feels a sense of relief and quietly thanks his lucky stars that all ended well.

The pessimist dreads challenges because he does not take full credit for his successes or failures. When things don't go his way, there are almost always circumstances that contributed that were beyond his control.

Strangely enough, the word *hope* becomes an action word. That is, hope requires more than simply wishing for the best, as in the case of the pessimist, but instead entails working toward that end, as in the case of the optimist.

Yet one's own individual experiences do not entirely expose the whole picture. Often one is influenced indirectly. That is to say, one does not have to solely realize positive or negative outcomes themselves but instead can be exposed to an environment that fosters such ideals of optimism or pessimism. Given this condition, often either one can be engrained in the minds of the impressionable and can ultimately create a self-fulfilling prophecy. That is to say, those who expect a positive outcome are more inclined to see the positive attributes in any outcome based upon their predisposition. And those who expect less than a positive outcome tend to focus on those particulars, which would confirm their predisposition.

Unfortunately, in cases of this nature, only after years of life experiences and education will one obtain some semblance of objectivity.

In my experiences, I can think of only one other area that contributes to either of the two perspectives. This area has to do with biological, chemical imbalances within the individual. Given the degree of the imbalance, one can range from dangerous, unrealistic optimism to equally dangerous levels of paranoia and depression. Fortunately, because of the abnormal behavior associated with these forms of optimism and pessimism, they are more rare.

Thus, because most cases are cases of psychological training versus physiological abnormalities, it is my belief that given the choice, one would choose to affiliate with those who would allow the best opportunity to continue to learn and grow. That being said, I believe one can learn from each of these perspectives but unfortunately not nearly in equal amounts. For it is the optimist who allows for greater expansive learning because of his innate ability to take chances, confront challenges, and accept changes more readily.

The matter becomes more of a question of not the man who is subject to the toss of a coin but rather the man who believes in a greater power. And I believe the optimistic man relies on that greater power—a power that evens out the wrongs and rights of the world, a power that rules with fairness, a power that gives man hope. And I am certain when I say that that power lies within each man and that he chooses whether or not to utilize it. For that power is free agency.

Imagine for a moment a world without hope . . .

Better yet, choose optimism, and you choose to open the door to the seemingly impossible.

Enlightenment

It is in darkness that we learn to see.

January 30, 1999

❧

Periods of Silence

There are periods of silence . . .   that hark of an angel's voice.
There are moments of bliss . . .   white as the drone of noise.
There is peace . . .   within the simple freedom of choice.

There are periods of silence . . .   that scream of rage and strife.
There are moments of bliss . . .   still shared between a husband and a wife.
There is peace . . .   amid the tragedies in life.

There are periods of silence . . .   empty as a single chair.
There are moments of bliss . . .   tender as a mother's care.
There is peace . . .   more abundant than it is rare.

There are periods of silence . . .   deafening with anticipation.
There are moments of bliss . . .   in a tearful reconciliation.
There is peace . . .   after the struggle of emancipation.
There are periods of silence . . .   as the babes are finally at rest.
There are moments of bliss . . .   watching the bluebird build its nest.
There is peace . . .   when the heart is at its best.

There are periods of silence . . .   faintly present near the break of dawn.
There are moments of bliss . . .   fragile as the feeble fawn.
There is peace . . .   Embrace it before it's gone.

There are periods of silence . . .
There are moments of bliss . . .
There is peace . . .

May 18, 2001

Time

12:16 p.m.
The first time,
Midnight, Greenwich mean,
Pastime—
It's about time.

Summertime,
The new year, yesterday,
Halftime,
A decade, an hour—
The right time.

An age, the era,
Sometime,
Centuries, a blink,
Minute by minute—
In the meantime.

Monday, November,
Crunch time,
One week, two months—
Timeliness.

Do you have the time?

Sunset, sunrise,
On time,
For the moment, timeless,

Tomorrow—
End of time.

Present, future,
Sands of time,
Before time, millennia,
Tick-tock—
Step in time.

Every time, at the time,
Now and then,
Anytime,
Forever, today—
Out of time.

Final seconds, overtime,
"Time's up,"
In the nick of time,
Eternity, the past—
Just in time.

Time out.

What time is it?

December 31, 1999

Trust

December 24, 1999

Few words can match the significance of trust in human relationships. It is the building block of all relationships. And like a building block, it will be put through many stress tests in a lifetime, causing a teetering effect with each new stressor.

In our initial stages of life, the foundational cornerstone block is laid. With healthy parenting, a child will begin to develop a sound understanding of trust. As the child grows, he is constantly receiving feedback and confirmation from the parent. Although the child may be unaware that he is testing trust, he is simply looking for the consistency within the boundaries that have been set by his parents.

It is only through repeated violations of this consistency that a child begins to stop and question the rules to the relationship and, to a larger extent, his perception of the stability of the world around him. Without that initial dose of trust established by the time a child reaches his minor years, he is set out into the world on an endless quest for that which cannot be fully recaptured. Often he will begin to set up defenses to compensate for the fearful place he now perceives the world to be.

I proffer that it is our innate predisposition to trust, anthropologically given to life by a set of parents who will take great strides to ensure our well-being and safety to protect the furtherance of the bloodline and species. We come into this world with total vulnerability and are literally subject to the whims of our parents. We seek safety in the arms of our parents and trust that they will do right by us.

It is this trust gleaned from our parents that we extend to our human relationships. Yet perhaps it is our own naiveté that leads us to believe that all people share the same experience with trust. We somehow forget that each person has been exposed to their own set of building blocks and experiences. Where there is an opportunity to trust, we often mistakenly substitute faith, faith that mankind will do what is morally and ethically correct or in the best interest of one another. And in as much as that is an optimistic view, it is not a certainty.

Trust, although inherent in our biology, is built over time. As with our parents, consistency within a person's character and behavior will provide the predictability and accountability that we seek in others to trust and feel a sense of safety. After a trusting relationship has been established, trust cognitively rarely enters the relationship. For only when an individual whom we have come to know does something out of character that violates our understanding of who they are is it brought out into the light. And it is upon repeated violations that our trust begins to teeter and may eventually fall.

Though you may lose your trust in a particular person, most people do not extend that loss beyond that relationship. Yet it is often in our significant relationships where our trust has been betrayed that we withhold trust for extended periods and beyond the immediate relationship. We refrain from putting ourselves into situations where long-term or lasting trust becomes a part of the required interaction. Safety and vulnerability are now paramount because of the great pain and disappointment the betrayal has caused us, and only time and a return to consistent behavior can alleviate those concerns.

Finally, mutual trust is the foundation of all thriving and lasting relationships. There is no substitute. And as much as one would desire to build and share in such a wonderful lifelong endeavor where reliance free from dependency exists on a level playing field, I leave you with this caution: it is doubly difficult to repair broken trust than it is to maintain a healthy one.

Avoidance

Given the option . . . I'd rather not choose.

February 2, 1998

Extremes

To raise a son like his father did
Is to suffocate one with too much burden.
To raise his son at the other end
Is to lose his son to the relentless wind.

Water that is cooled is soon not water
But transferred as another entity.
Water that is heated is soon not there
But circulating somewhere in the air.

To be addicted to a specific trail
Is as wrong as to have no direction.
As the narrow-minded have limited views,
The overly broad-minded simply can't choose.

The one who fasts and refuses to eat
Soon finds himself lying flat on the ground,
But the one who continues and overindulges
Finds himself just as paralyzed by unwelcome bulges.

June 17, 1986

Gossip

A living, breathing, contagious disease easily
curable with the application of a button.

September 17, 1999

Life's Lessons

May 8, 1999

There are simple things in life that most people gravitate toward. Then there are the more complex things that fewer take hold of. Don't push aside the simple things; they will most definitely keep you grounded. And don't shy away from the more complex; they will define who you are.

Challenge yourself to be better, to be one more open, one more patient, one more forgiving, one more compassionate, one more understanding, one more loving, one more giving, and one more healthy.

Love life, respect life, and create life, and you will give life meaning.

Look deep into the eyes of another, and you will see life . . . with all its flaws and glory.

Kiss babies and inhale their hope and promise.

Give to our senior citizens the same tenderness you give to a child. (June 25, 1999)

Appreciate the rainbow of personalities, and you will accept the difference between black and white. (June 25, 1999)

There is no obstacle greater than fear. (June 30, 1999)

True acceptance searches for no one, for it is blind. (July 1, 1999)

So rare are the true ones. (July 9, 1999)

Imperfection is the perfect example of mankind. (July 9, 1999)

Big brothers make a difference. (July 9, 1999)

Where there is compromise, there is advancement. (September 8, 1999)

Where there is stubbornness, there is suppression. (September 8, 1999)

To participate is the first step to your success. (September 8, 1999)

Compromise is addition through subtraction. (September 17, 1999)

There is no substitute for a solid foundation. (September 17, 1999)

There is immeasurable growth each day. (September 17, 1999)

In every **hear**tache, there is an ear to listen to your pain. (September 29, 1999)

Evil cannot penetrate a true heart. (August 3, 1999)

Love is . . . beyond explanation. (October 15, 1999)

Dreams are pools of endless possibilities; dive in and immerse yourself in all that you dare to imagine. (March 8, 2000)

Equality—ask not for more than you are willing to give. (December 25, 2000)

You risk only that with which you have already departed. (December 25, 2000)

Insignificance is a matter of opinion. Significance is a matter of desire. (December 25, 2000)

Freedom is overcoming your fears. (April 12, 2001)

Acceptance can truly only come from within. (April 12, 2001)

Addiction—the epitome of a love–hate relationship. (May 28, 2001)

There is nothing brighter than a child's smile. (May 28, 2001)

"Then" contains so much more than "now" and so much less than "when." (October 31, 2002)

Within each life, there comes a pause. What you make of it will be impactful. (October 31, 2002)

Not deciding may be your biggest decision ever. (October 31, 2002)

The last word often lasts. (October 31, 2002)

Some of the most successful people in the world have tasted their share of defeat. Some of the most defeated people in the world have tasted success. The ultimate difference may simply be linked to desire. (November 29, 2002)

The eldest child has the burden of the family values. (November 29, 2002)

To question your ability is to increase the odds of your failure. (December 5, 2002)

To think about tomorrow puts the present in the past. (January 4, 2008)

To relive yesterday lessens today. (January 4, 2008)

Every grain of sand that falls builds the island that is you. (January 4, 2008)

The mere thought of what I don't know teaches me more than I'll ever know. (January 4, 2008)

Silence is a golden hue. (January 4, 2008)

Sadness lacks appreciation. (January 4, 2008)

Rage is the beautiful storm where harmony lives. Open your heart and put aside your fears. (January 4, 2008)

To rage is to experience your past, present, and future all at once. (January 4, 2008)

To be without thought transcends the idea. (January 4, 2008)

Every key I press leads me onward to the next. (January 4, 2008)

Appreciation should never go unnoticed. (January 4, 2008)

Each year, the tree reminds us that life is a circle and that all that is will be again. (January 4, 2008)

Forgiveness breaks the chains. (January 4, 2008)

Obsession is slavery. (January 4, 2008)

True forgiveness is liberating. (January 4, 2008)

An audience goes away, as should the feeling they imbue. (January 4, 2008)

The best advice may yet have been proffered. (January 4, 2008)

The healthiest person is the one you love. (January 4, 2008)

Mistakes can be corrected if you are willing to acknowledge them. (January 4, 2008)

Time without reference doesn't exist. (January 4, 2008)

Happiness is more than an emotion. It is a state of being. (January 4, 2008)

You can't teach one how to be happy. You can only reflect its glow. (January 4, 2008)

When expectations are low, disappointment doesn't taste as bad. (May 1, 2008)

Low expectations digest disappointment with ease. (May 1, 2008)

It's easiest to excuse those for whom your expectations never amounted. (May 1, 2008)

Happiness is . . . enough, not more. (November 7, 2008)

Realism is claimed by those who refuse to consider or validate another perspective. (November 20, 2008)

Ignorance can be a learned trait. (October 20, 2009)

The handwritten letter conveys so much more than the keyboard can express. (October 20, 2009)

Perfection is an endless search. (January 8, 2010)

Please direct me to perfection as my GPS can't seem to locate it. (January 12, 2010)

Some of the greatest challenges do not end in success as it would be measured by data but rather measured by what you learn. (March 1, 2010)

It's not how we agree that defines us but how we disagree. (April 15, 2010)

The greatest leaders are. (April 15, 2010)

Mercy is the ultimate sign of self-respect. (April 15, 2010)

Good leaders are not those who know how to agree but rather those who know how to respectfully disagree. (May 7, 2010)

An old man's vision is not measured in feet but rather in years. (September 12, 2012)

You seldom find what you are not looking for. (May 1, 2013)

The collective strengths of our differences make us better. (May 24, 2013)

Every breath I take leads me to my last. (May 24, 2013)

I've never felt more pressure than that which I've placed upon myself. (May 24, 2013)

Relationships, like flowers, require regular watering. (May 24, 2013)

I don't know if I've ever had a unique thought. But I know it is mine, which leads me to wonder if the same idea can be discovered more than once, each idea completely independent of one another. (May 24, 2013)

Blame can destroy a teaching moment. (June 20, 2013)

My life is a reflection of every soul that's touched it, some more than others. The greatest decisions I've made have been informed by others. (June 1, 2014)

Knowing my weaknesses makes me stronger. (June 1, 2014)

Every compliment improves the chances of world peace. (June 1, 2014)

Elevating another's perception of themselves elevates their perception of you. (June 1, 2014)

Gratification is . . . watching others sing your song. (June 1, 2014)

There are few shortcuts in life worth taking; prepare for the road less traveled. (2018)

Habits require repeated practice. (2018)

Nothing soothes the soul like accomplishing a goal. (2018)

Earning your awards is that much more rewarding. (2018)

Life—What a Bitch

Things don't always go
According to the plan,
And sometimes that is
What's hard to understand.

Things don't always go
The way you want them to,
And throughout your life, you'll find
That this is also true.

Things don't always work out
As you thought they would,
Even though you know
You've tried the best you could.

But you must not give up
Even though it's knocked you down.
Just get back on your feet
'Cause there's still another round

And soon, you'll find
You've heard enough of all this shit.
And this is when you say,
"Fuck it. I quit!"

April 19, 1984

Mescaline

Do you sometimes feel you're **slipping** from reality,
Living in a world of **confusion**,
Searching for your own personality,
And **suddenly**, it's so amusing?

Do you sometimes feel you're on the **outside** looking in,
Every day **losing** a step or two,
A stranger to the **ever-changing** winds,
And everything **looks** so new?

Do you sometimes **wonder** if there's life after death,
Contemplating hidden **answers**,
Listening to your e ve ry br ea th,
And **reflecting** on all the cancers?

Do you sometimes **feel** you've been here before,
Glaring into a **crystal** ball,
Still having no **control** for what's in store,
And the axe is about to **fall**?

Do you sometimes feel you're running from the **shadows**
Reaching and **clawing** at your back?
All of a sudden, the feeling **goes**,
And the blue sky turns to **black**.

September 25, 1983

Pathetic

An abused runaway clasps himself while inhaling a cigarette on a brisk winter's early morning dawn, contemplating the welfare of his younger siblings.

As the sky above is illuminated by the hidden virgin sun, a weary hunchbacked bag lady struggles to free a coin wedged between the crack of a rusted manhole cover.

Down the empty streets, oblivious to the world around them, those imprisoned by their thoughts wander aimlessly, sputtering angry words at their invisible adversaries.

Tripping in her high heels, another father's little princess grapples in her purse for her mother's misplaced lipstick to entice any man to love her for a price.

A discarded, mangy mutt claws through a tipped trash can, hoping to fill the void between his cage-like skeletal ribs, all the while aware of the ferocious predators lurking behind.

Peacefully, there you are,
Asleep and sound,
The warmth of wool
Hidden behind bolted doors,
Enclosed with security alarms,
Taken by the nightmare.
It's impossible to decide—
Cashmere or corduroy.

October 15, 1995

The Stranger

Not knowing where she was going,
She knew that the time was near.
Someone was watching her carefully.
She could sense that chilling air.

Lost in an unknown city,
Walking down an empty street,
She felt someone behind her.
All she heard were distant feet.

She turned only to see darkness.
She knew someone was there.
Her lips began to tremble
As she was overcome with fear.

She ran down a dark alley,
As fast as she could move her feet.
All sounds around were silenced
By the pounding of her heartbeat.

She noted a black shadow
Growing larger on the wall.
She heard some heavy breathing.
She got on her knees to crawl.

The footsteps got much closer
As she fled behind a box.

From where she crouched, she saw his shoes,
So she felt the ground for rocks.

He placed his hand on her shoulder
As she let out a piercing scream.
She opened her eyes, and her mother said,
"Honey, it was only a dream."

January 31, 1984

The Truth Hurts

Spoken clearly without thought,
Razor-sharp as winter's breeze,
It may not be what you sought,
Yet excuse me, if you please.

My tongue, which has no fingers,
Is free to release the truth.
Regret may be what lingers
And guilt for a lack of couth.

Yet if conscience played a part,
Will the truth then not be told?
It's born strictly from the heart
Without the chance to grow too old.

But what has me more confused
Is the shock that's in your eyes.
There's a sense that I've been used
In the need to tell you lies.

December 9, 1998

The Being

I can try and try but only dent the wall,
Then I attempt again, only to be stalled,

And once I stop, it rebuilds itself.

And once again, it restores itself.

It seems as though
Yet it doesn't seem to understand

If I break through, all will fall,
I'll be there to help.

It's protecting

Something that will die

Something strong and extremely powerful,

Or shrivel away if ever revealed.

It's difficult
That there are areas of gray,

To make this being understand
That it's okay to make mistakes.

If only I could

Maybe a little at a time

Let a beam of light through the wall,

Will start to fall.

As it falls, it energizes the being
It can remain in control,

So when fully exposed,
Stand on its own.

It's a dangerous task.

For if I let too much light in at once

It should be done with extreme care.

The being will burn!

April 6, 1985

The Thief of the Night

I finally found my way to bed after an early rise had left me exhausted.
My pillow's familiar scent welcomed me, comforted me.
As I relished a deep, full breath, it embraced my head, and my arms
reciprocated the sensuous tender emotion.
At last, I may rest . . .

A minute passes.

I turn my cheek to the other side, thinking this will be more comfortable.
I rub my eye and brush the residue from my face.
How good it feels to be in bed, I think to myself. *In moments, I'll be fast
asleep.*

Tick, tick, tick, tick . . .

I can't believe I can hear that clock in the other room from here.
I turn my head back over, knowing I'm always more comfortable facing
this direction.

A couple of minutes pass.

Now the pillow is beginning to get too hot, so I flip it over to rest my
face against the cooler side.
Ah, much better. It's only a matter of time now as I check the red
numbers of my bedside alarm clock to see how much sleep I'll get before
I must rise again.

I lightly close my eyes.
My pillow smells so good.
Another deep breath, a sigh . . .

A moment.

Then my eyes pop open, staring directly at those damn bright red numbers.
I squint, get my eyes focused, close them again, and then reopen them quickly to check the time once more.
After several more times of this useless exercise, I decide to change positions.

I now take on what I call my vampire position.
I lie flat on my back with my arms resting lightly across my chest, as if to protect my heart from the wooden stake.
My legs are straightened except for the overlap at the crossing of my ankles (so I'm a comfortable vampire).
I think to myself, *It's not as cozy*, but at times, this position has been effective.

I close my eyes again, take an agitated breath, and leave it up to the air to find its way out of my slightly parted lips.
At last, I may rest . . . I hope.

Several minutes actually pass.

I am now ever so conscious of every sprinkle of light, every minute sound, and the actual weight of the blankets draped over my toes.
Those little red numbers have now illuminated the entire room.
The five-dollar kitchen clock seems to be having delusions of grandeur, and everybody in the city has decided to take a midnight drive—down my block!

Now I'm angry and wide awake, and the only thing I can think of is how much sleep I'm not getting!

I regroup and figure it's got to be some Zen thing and I need to complete some unfinished business. So I go over the day's events, mentally stopping at the high points and giving each a fair amount of contemplation— nothing noted.

Now I begin to run through tomorrow's calendar of important appointments—and aha! That's it! I forgot to make a note of a birthday card I need to pick up for a coworker. So I scamper out of bed and go to the kitchen to write down the reminder.

While there, I take advantage of the opportunity and grab a glass of water, gulp it down, and give the clock on the wall (which has mysteriously quieted) a scowl. Then I trudge on back to my room, satisfied that I have now addressed all unfinished business and would easily fall asleep.

As I climb into bed, I glare at the alarm clock and realize another half hour has passed. I try to rationalize to myself that it was time well spent but not buying it for a minute.
I curl up, firmly grab the blanket, and yank it to my neck as there has been a notable cooling of the temperature in the room.
I press my face firmly against my pillow in an effort to warm it to my liking, breathe in its familiar scent, and close my eyes, praying that at last, I might sleep.

Now I toss and turn for a good forty-five minutes and vow to myself that I would not get up. But I could not keep that confounded promise. As I peer over at the clock, there are only four and a half restless hours 'til that alarm would go off, and I'm not a bit sleepy.

Well, I clench the blanket and throw it off in one quick swoosh, jump out of bed, turn on the light, snatch my robe, and head down the end of the hallway to the den. Once there, I flick on the light switch, grab my pen and paper, and sit down to write.

Two and a half hours later, I stomp on back to my room, toss my robe aside, jump into my bed, snag the blanket and pull it over my head, put the pillow in a headlock, and plead with no one that I may fall asleep.

Oh, one last thing . . .
I bet you'll never guess what I wrote about.

September 25, 1999

Song for Gene

Round and Round

December 19, 2020

Round and round
Here we go
Round and round
Here we go again

Round and round
Here we go
Round and round
Here we go again

Running circles in my mind
Back and forth again
Are we running out of time
Are we coming to an end

We've been down this road before
Time and time again
But I can't do this anymore
We're far beyond the bend

And we go . . .
Round and round
Here we go
Round and round
Here we go again

Help me
Find a way
To tell your heart goodbye

'Cause I can't bear to see you cry
It's tearing me apart (over and again)
We've done all we can to try
Is it time for us to part (it's so hard to comprehend)

And we go round and round
Round and round, we go
Here we go again
Round and round

Instrumental

Bridge

We said it would be forever
Made plans beyond tomorrow
Oh . . . what happened to
Me and you

We fight, make love, we holler
We laugh, we cry, say sorry
Is it true
Are we through

Round and round
Here we go
Round and round
Here we go again

Tell me
There's a way
Not to tell your heart goodbye

Can we give it one more try
And I go round and round
Round and round, I go
Round and round
Here I go again
On this merry-go-round
Over and again
Over and again
Over and again

An Appreciation
of Life

Through Dying Eyes

January 3

First, I must admit I find it quite strange that I am speaking to an empty book whose purpose at this time escapes me. So please forgive me if I am at a loss, for I am still ambivalent about this endeavor and do not know for how long I will continue. You see, I've never given much thought to writing and frankly less thought to keeping a diary. Yet she insisted it would comfort me in times of need. And though there have been so . . . so many sleepless nights, I'm not quite clear why it is now that I have chosen to take her advice. I hope it is with time that this lack of clarity comes into focus.

On another note, I am unsure of how to address you, who may become my closest friend since my wife's passing on. "Dear" seems so personal and was always a word reserved for her and her alone. Perhaps I'll give this some more thought.

Well, having said that, I'll rest until I am so inclined to write again.

January 6

Well, here we are again. What is it that you want to hear? Should I tell you how my day was? Would you like to know what I had for dinner or if there is a new fling in my life, or is it that you want to hear me cry and tell you how much I miss her?

Oh, I know; you want to know how I'm feeling. You want to know what's on my mind. How I'm coping. Listen, I'm just doing this for her, and right now, I'm not seeing any benefit in this. As a matter of fact,

I'm not too sure I even care to continue with this foolishness. So, my so-called friend, back in the drawer you go.

January 9

This is crazy. I haven't got the faintest idea of what I'm doing. I don't even know where to start.

Here. How's this? The days last forever and the nights even longer. I've questioned why I've been left alone to deal with this torturous agony. I've asked myself over and again what I've done to deserve such a fate. And at times, I feel so selfish and pitiful for asking. I've gone in circles, walking aimlessly around the house, over who is to blame. There are no answers. My emotions have all but been depleted.

As I sit here writing, I can't help but wonder what more tomorrow will bring. Sometimes I wish whoever controls this game we call "life" would just let me out. But I know deep within my heart that's not the man I am. And I fear the thought that somehow, somewhere, she might be watching me and shaking her head at the slightest hint that I would want to quit. So I press on . . . Is that what you want to hear, damn it?

How would you feel if you had to look at an empty chair for the rest of your life? How would you feel if you had to be reminded every time a piece of junk mail arrives? How would you feel if every goddamn time the house settles, your heart stops, and you don't know whether to shit or scream? How would you feel? You tell me how you would feel, goddamn it!

January 10

Can we start over? I've just reread my past entries, and I don't like how any of this sounds. It's not usually like me to sound so despondent, so angry, and I'm finding it's not as easy as I thought it was going to be, writing about what I'm doing or how I'm feeling. You have to understand. For the better part of my life, I've been trained not to show any emotions or vulnerabilities. It's been survival for me.

Let me explain. I'm a retired cop who put in thirty-plus years dealing daily with more ugliness and despicableness than the average person ever sees in a lifetime. And to just open up and let all that out, which has been sealed up for so long, really seems . . . Well, let's just say I don't know if I can do it. I need time. Just give me some time.

I'll try . . . okay?

Thanks. Until next time.

January 12

Let's start this way . . . I woke up a little late this morning and took my walk at 7:00 a.m. The hustle and bustle of cars and horns had already begun and made for a noisy start to my day. So I cut it short, went back inside, and sat in front of the television, flipping through the channels until I fell back asleep. She hated when I'd do that. She used to say it was a waste of the day, but these days, my energy isn't what it used to be. Anyway, it's not like she's gonna say anything now.

Oh, this is ridiculous . . . I don't know why I'm wasting my time telling you about this stuff. What good is this really doing?

January 13

You know, I was thinking a lot today . . . Maybe this existence is made to be painful so we can all use our imagination and create a place to look forward to where there is no more pain. Or maybe pain only hurts because we acknowledge it. I don't know; I'm just talking. I've been asking a lot of crazy questions these days. Like I said before, there just doesn't seem to be any answers.

The one thing I'm gradually coming to know is that I'm getting tired.

Tired of the pain and tired of always feeling angry—like I'm ready to explode. It doesn't appear to be getting me anywhere anymore. And I'm not so sure that it ever really did. Although the one thing I am becoming increasingly sure of is I don't like what I'm becoming, which is a bitter old man.

I'm reminding myself of my childhood when as youths, my friends and I would stay away from that cranky old man who lived on the corner. He never seemed to smile but instead had a constant furrow across his brow, and he'd snap at us every time we'd retrieve our ball from his yard. Then one day the fire trucks and ambulance came, carried him away, and we never saw him again. I never dreamed I'd turn out like him and don't want to be remembered like that. Though now I wonder which cards life had dealt him . . .

January 16

Today has been like many others before it. I find myself still searching . . . Although I know she is gone, she is still around every corner I turn and in everything I see. While at the grocery store this afternoon, I saw this woman down the aisle whom I would have bet any amount of money was she. She had the same soft build, shape, hair color, and no-fuss, easy style. The simple grandmotherly dress she wore could have been pulled from her wardrobe, and her tiny tennis shoes were the same color, a light lavender. She even squeezed and held the loaf just as my wife would, firm but not so much as to damage its shape. I just stared, frozen where I stood, and watched from a distance until she finally turned and disappeared at the end of the aisle.

Now intellectually, I knew it could not be her, but I was compelled to put aside my immediate interests in the bread and pastry aisle to confirm what I already knew. As I went around the other end of the aisle, I cautiously but intently observed this woman, engrossed in her every move. When I finally passed her going in the opposite direction, it was plainly obvious that she was not my wife. And I didn't know if I was to feel saddened or relieved. I felt both. Yet for the remainder of my shopping, I continually looked for that woman in every part of the store.

Last week, while in line at the movie theater, I had a similar experience. I heard a sweet chuckle from behind that I could have sworn was hers. I casually turned so as not to make it look obvious. To my shock, the woman, who was a couple of people behind me, was this much older woman who didn't, in the least, look like her. But when I turned back to face the front of the line, her chuckle was unmistakably hers.

It's like I'm going crazy. All of a sudden, I feel a connection with these mere strangers; I hold them warmly within my heart simply because they remind me of her. I find I automatically attribute all the goodness that she was to them. Is that odd? Is it that I desire to see her so desperately that suddenly, everyone looks and sounds like her, or have they always been there, and I've never really paid attention? Whichever the case, I'm still left longing.

January 20

It's happened again. Someone called and asked for a "William," and when I heard the voice, it sounded so much like her. But when I told her she'd reached the wrong number, she apologized and hung up before I had the chance to ask, "Who's calling?" This is the third time she's misdialed in the past month. I keep thinking it's a practical joke, but if it is, I can't think of anyone who could be so cruel. Does she know what she's doing to me?

I get so angry, my heart races, and my blood boils. Then I take a minute, take a few breaths, stop, and wonder and hope she misdials again. I just want to talk to her and ask her how she is doing and tell her how much I hurt when she hung up so abruptly. I only want to hear her voice a little longer . . . I confess I sat for nearly an hour waiting for the phone to ring again before I realized the ludicrousness of my actions.

January 21

I came upon an article today about living with someone who is dying. (Ironically, it was in the "Living" section of the paper.) It spoke of the stages of dying and how an outsider can recognize when the final days are nearing. It stated that you could see it in their eyes: the fatigue and the capitulation. It spoke of the denial, anger, depression, questioning, and acceptance. Though I don't know if I buy all of it. She seemed to take most of it with a pretty good demeanor. Yes, there were times when she was depressed. But who wouldn't be? What I remember most was her positive attitude. I can't recall a single time when I saw her angry. Now me? Yes, I am angry, and I have a million questions.

You know, sometimes I wonder where they get the people who write this crap.

January 24

Damn it! I can't believe that some people have no consideration. I've been mulling over this all day. I stepped out to grab my morning paper and found another pile of dog shit on my lawn. Where the hell are the leash laws in this community? I know it was the Branighans' dog; they never put that son-of-a-bitch mutt on a leash. I've had to scare him off too many times. One of these days, I swear. I spent the better part of my day trying to figure out if I ought to go over there and give them a piece of my mind, along with their dog's shit, or poison the little bastard. Damn it, what is this world coming to?

And another thing: I'm getting tired of all this junk mail. Don't these people have anything better to do than throw knives at people? Where's the compassion? Where's the sensitivity? Where's the idiotic, simple common courtesy?

January 26

I spent the day just moping around the house, going stir-crazy. The dishes are clean, the bed is made, and not a pillow on the sofa is out of place. I need something to occupy my time, but I don't want to feel like I'm trying to replace her; nothing could replace her.

It feels like eternity, dealing with this. It's slowly eating away at me, and I know thinking about it only makes it worse. How long? That's all I want to know. How long?

February 1

My mind was preoccupied, as usual. Though today I believe it was mostly positive but somewhat bittersweet. I was recalling when we were young and walking along the beach in Monterey. It was hot all afternoon during our walk down Cannery Row, but we made our way to the beach just as the sun was going down. We stood at the face of the Pacific and watched as the sun slowly lowered itself under the gentle giants' cool blanket. And right before its last ray was put to rest, she softly told me that she loved me for the first time. She was so overcome with emotion; she squeezed me tightly.

I too felt the butterflies of love and adrenaline racing through my body. I held on to her and told her that I loved her too and that like the sun, even when darkness came, I'd always be beaming because I had her in my heart. She smiled at me with love in her eyes. Then we both began to laugh, partly out of the sheer nervousness and endorphins running through us and mostly at my poor attempt to be poetic.

Later, when I took her home that evening, I knew she had touched a part of me that no other gal had ever come close to, and I hoped that someday she'd be my wife—if she'd give me the honor.

One year later, we were married on that very beach.

February 2

Last night, I told you about a very special time in my life, probably the most special, and I'm not quite sure why I shared that. There aren't many more people around with which I share such personal memories. It's got me thinking and asking myself why I have been so private about my feelings and issues. I know I've done it to myself to a greater extent, but I'm not so sure it's been the most prudent thing to do.

I must say, after last night's entry, I kind of felt like it was okay. Like maybe getting some of this stuff out is helpful. It's even strange that although I've only been writing for a month, I can feel myself relaxing, becoming more comfortable with talking about myself. I'll have to give this some more thought because on the other hand, I'm kind of queasy about being so explicit with my life.

Oh, well. Sooner or later, I'm sure you'll be the first to know if and when I'm ready to open up and tell all.

February 5

Anger—what an emotion. It's been increasingly on my mind for the past few days. I've been consumed by it for as long as I can remember. Why? I don't know. Even before her death, it lived within me, accompanying so many of my decisions. For the greater part of my life, I knew it was there but ignored its powerful influence. It's only now, when I have been writing, that I am beginning to really sense its impact or, rather, its absence. I'd like to blame the police work for igniting its flame, and although I can't ignore that cops live in an environment where anger breathes and breeds, I have to acknowledge that somehow I am responsible.

She used to tell me that if I didn't control my temper, one day it would get the best of me. Believe me, there were many days when it almost ended my career: from dealing with the dirtbags to dealing with department politics. Before, it was easy to shove it back; there were life's distractions and day-to-day living that always had to take precedence. But now I'm finding that this is the greatest test of all:

having to live alone with anger. And sadly, I'm seeing what she had to endure throughout our lives together.

It's hard to believe that she never got up and left me for a better man. I know I wouldn't and couldn't stand for me that long. Hell, this year's been long enough. And it is only now that I am beginning to fully understand the significance of what "getting the best of me" really means.

Maybe there's a crack in my stubbornness that's widening that compels me now to choose how I intend on living the rest of my life. Maybe it's the fear of failure that has so often flowed side by side with the anger. Or possibly, it's getting a taste of how life could be without the anger, but probably, it's a fair amount of all of them put together. Whichever the combination, I now know that anger is not the way.

February 6

We used to talk about how it would be when that time finally came. She apologized a hundred times for her illness. She asked me to be strong while allowing me to be weak. The truth is we took turns being strong for each other. There were times near the end when she didn't have the will to rise in the morning, so we'd both lie in bed, savoring the little time we had left together.

Those times meant so much but hurt even more deeply, simply because I knew we were running out of time. I used to fear that she'd never awake in the morning, and when she did, I was so grateful. But then seeing her in such pain made me feel guilty for asking for another day. I wonder how long she hung on just for me. And from time to time, that thought eats at me. How much more pain did I cause her to endure?

It was such a difficult time. I'd never wish something like that upon my worst enemy.

February 12

A week has passed since my last entry, and though I have done a lot of thinking, I must admit I didn't give much thought to writing. Maybe too much shame, I don't know, but definitely some soul-searching.

Yet today there was a burning pain inside that compelled me to seek your ear. The truth is I needed to share with someone and didn't have anyone. I have spent endless nights talking to her, cursing her, asking her why she left me, and telling her how much I need her as if she still lies beside me, but I'm realizing the seasons have revolved, and my mind can no longer continue with this madness.

So I arranged her weekly bouquet with freshly cut crimson roses, baby's breath, and a couple of lemon tree blossoms. I inhaled deeply its sweet floral scent and made my final journey to her gravesite. As I trudged up the rolling hillside, I had to stop a bit to catch my breath. The cold winter air stung the tips of my ears and reminded me how sharply painful this lonely existence is. My breath met the silvery mist with its own plume of dissipating life. And the afternoon drizzle fell lightly among the damp, dark black and forest-green cypress, adding to the weight that filled my already heavy heart.

While I prepared the fertile soil, my mind recalled how, in her final days, she encouraged me to find another companion. It was just like her to still worry about me up until the bitter end. We would laugh, joke, and sarcastically list all the women who would want an old stubborn fart like me. Then we'd cling to each other and wait for time to cease. But we were always given another day. That was until a year ago today.

She is still so much a part of me, and I promised her that she would always be. As I stood there, I told her how sorry I was for carrying so much anger for so long and for allowing so much time to be wasted when it is so precious. I promised her that I would try to be a better man, one whom she could be proud of again. I wept for some time, pouring my heart out to her until I couldn't cry anymore. Then I carefully separated the roses just so and forlornly watched as the drizzle coated them with its frosty dew. It was so hard to just walk away.

Before I left, I pressed my lips to my fingers and gently ran them across the engraved letters of her name, feeling each ridge until they slid off the smooth end, dripping from the wetness that had accumulated. I turned from her white granite headstone, headed back down the wet hillside, and didn't look back. It hurt too much to leave her, and steeling myself was the only way. Though now I wished I had one last time.

February 13

I awoke today with the morning half spent and the new day's bright amber light cascading through the break between the valance and the sheer window drapery. The night brought much-needed rest as I slowly rose and sat up to begin the rest of my life.

As I stood, I reached for the ceiling with both hands and stretched my usually stiff and aching body. Surprisingly, the joints seemed lubed, and the pains were few. I relaxed just long enough to sense a strange calm in the air. I stopped and paused for a moment in an attempt to identify it. I turned my head slightly, and suddenly, I became keenly aware of all my senses. A feeling came over me in what I can only describe as enlightenment. I felt and heard myself breathe for the first time in . . . I can't remember how long. I watched as my chest rose and fell, and I remember my shoulders feeling as if the world had been lifted from them. I closed my eyes gently and allowed a warm love to surround and permeate my open heart.

Immediately, I knew she was here with me. I felt her with all my being and could sense the air of her presence. Somewhere between she and me, there was an electricity that connected us. Within it, there was peace, understanding, and a brilliant, golden love. I held on to it with earnest affection as it wrapped itself around me, comforting and encouraging, until it gradually faded from my senses. And all that remained was a light fragrance of her dancing in the air. My face and heart smiled warmly with the greatest joy and loving affection burning within as a tear of genuine happiness welled in my eye and rolled down my aging face. It was then that I knew she would always be beside me.

Before heading into the shower, I grabbed her bathrobe, which I had never removed from its hook since her passing, brought it to my nose, deeply inhaled her fading, sweet scent once again, and brought her back to life for the moment. It always makes me feel as if she were not far away but still here, where she belongs. Though now I was certain she was still here, somewhere, watching over me.

While I stood beneath the shower's weak flow, I was ever cognizant as the soothing water seeped into my hair. Its warm wetness melted over my scalp, flowed over my face and lips, and streamed down my body. Goosebumps rose throughout my body as it acclimated itself to the temperature of the water. The metallic scent and flavor of the water was more sharp and pungent than I could ever recall. It came alive in my mouth as I swished it around my teeth, over my tongue, and spat it outward.

I thought, she always said this old house had a flavor of its own, and she used to beg me to get off my butt and replace that old showerhead. Though fixing stuff that still worked was never a priority and just another thing that I'd put off. And it seemed so useless to replace it after she was gone. Yet now I can't help but feel an urgency to repair all that I had ignored.

February 17

Not a lot going on around here the past few days. Just putting together a list of the things I need to do around the house to get things in order. Showerhead, plumber's tape, backyard sprinkler valve, PVC connectors, glue, cupboard wood stain, light bulbs, etc.

While I was rummaging through the basement, I was amazed by the amount of junk you can accumulate over a lifetime. Boy, the memories come rushing back. I found some old photo albums, my police academy graduation certificate, and an old diary of hers neatly packed away in a few dust-covered boxes. I spent a good hour or so reading various passages. It was stuffed with old notes I used to write to her when we had just fallen in love. I read this one letter that I had written in a card and noted what she wrote on the day she had received it. It really moved me and got me to thinking about who I was and who I've become.

I'd like to share them with you.

Here is what I wrote:

> Dearest love of mine,
>
> I spent the night thinking of you and the wonderful time we had at the fair. You looked so beautiful in your summer dress, and I felt like I was the luckiest man there. (Even though I wasn't able to win you that stuffed teddy bear.) You are always on my mind, and I can hardly wait to see you again. You have brought so much joy to my life, and I can't imagine living without you now that I've found you. I only hope I can make you as happy as you have made me. I love you forever.
>
> Love,
> Me

This is what she had written on the night that she received my letter:

> Dear Diary,
>
> Today I received a card from my love. It's hard to believe we've only been dating for six weeks. It seems as if I have known him all my life. We fit together like we

were always meant to be. I am so in love with him; my heart feels as large as a hot air balloon whenever we're together. He is the most wonderful and romantic man I could ever have dreamed of. He treats me like an angel, and he is so thoughtful. He is the most sensitive man I've ever met, and I secretly pray he will ask me to be his wife. My only fear is that he wants to be a police officer; I would just die if anything happened to him. Though I will support him with every ounce of my fiber because he means that much to me.

I can't wait to see him tomorrow and every day for the rest of my life.

It makes me wonder—whatever happened to the sensitive young man she speaks of? Life sure has a way of changing us, molding us. It's hard to believe that time really does wear on us all. Here, I thought I was this impenetrable rock of a man, self-assured, and independent from your everyday anybody. I really believed I had the answers to life's most difficult quandaries.

"People think too much," I used to tell her. "Life is not that difficult. Just keep it simple." I was so sure that there wasn't anything or anybody that could move me or persuade me to think differently. Now after all these years, I'm finally learning that time is the ever-persistent, silent adversary, slowly making of man what it will. And to think of all those wasted years. Though I know that young man is still alive somewhere within, lost in all this tragedy. He has to be. And I owe it to her to find him.

Well, I think I've said enough for now. I was simply trying to show you how much she meant to me and how much it hurts to be without her. Yet what I'm beginning to see is how selfish I've been. I can't believe how blind I've been. Somehow, somewhere, I've forgotten how much I meant to her. How she is feeling. How much she longs to be here with me. Maybe this is what I needed. To hear her voice, to actually see with my own two eyes the love that I have been taking for granted. (My dear, I'm so, so sorry. I will do better.)

February 19

I woke up today ready to take on the world and clean out the rest of the basement, but instead, I spent the morning poking around the dust until I got caught up looking through our old picture albums. *Where had all the years gone?* I thought. Every day seemed to be so trying at times. And getting through a week or a month seemed like an eternity. (Even today, now and then.)

Yet as I flipped from page to page, the years flew by. I realized there were many more good days than bad. I'm even smiling in some of the pictures. We were so young and she so beautiful. She always had a smile on her face and seemed completely comfortable wherever we were, even though I knew she would rather be somewhere else. It's only now that these photos bring about a joy within, and unfortunately, it's so bittersweet. It hurts not to be able to sit and share with her those memories. I wish I could have known then what I know now. I wish I could have appreciated then as much as I do now.

Later in the afternoon, after going down memory lane all morning, I took a hot shower and stood before the vanity for my shave. I couldn't help but look at the reflection and observe how time has passed. The lines deeper and the stubble silvery white. *Old* was the only word that came to mind.

March 1

Hello, my friend. I apologize for not having written in some time, but I needed to visit a friend who has been ill, and yet I have been true to my word as well. That is, I have been busy cleaning out old boxes of stuff and fixing things around the house, even though I'm not as nimble as I used to be. Anyhow, that old rusty-tasting shower is fresh as the mountain spring these days, and the water pressure is amazing! The cupboards have been reorganized and recoated with an antique white stain. And the unused canned goods have been prepared for the homeless. Everything is nearly in order. Yes, I have been productive.

The weather was so beautiful today. An early spring has definitely sprung, along with all the weeds in the garden, and how wonderfully green and new everything looks! I gassed up the old red Snapper and gave the lawn its first manicuring of the year. I hadn't realized how much energy it took to push through that thick grass, but the effort was well worth the unbelievable scent it released into the air. That palatable aroma of freshly cut bluegrass is so incredible and invigorating that I've begun to realize that life's simplest wonders are really something to behold.

The early daffodils with their bright yellow ribbons and the ruby-red tulips with their ends dipped in virgin-white cream against the rich dark chocolate–brown soil gave the afternoon such a picturesque, airy feeling of real beauty. I can't wait for them all to break through and reveal themselves. Even the sky seemed to raise its azure ceiling to allow for all the various shades of glorious green growth.

I spent the entire day absorbing the sun's rays while I methodically worked from one area of the yard to the other. My mind reflected on the years of tilling and sowing our future. The long swing and graveyard shifts with the department, promotions, and law enforcement politics. She was there through all the sleepless nights and every step of the way to encourage, counsel, and congratulate me.

I have always been the one who viewed the world as black and white, right or wrong, and she was the only one who could somehow show me gray. She had such an inner will and an undying belief in me. I miss her gentle strength and her tender touch, the way she would softly place her warm hand over my shoulder while I sat with my cigar and paper. It said so much without saying anything. Then time flew by, and retirement came so quickly. Soon, friends were few, yet she was always there.

I remember how she loved this time of the year. She'd spend whole days in the garden picking, pulling, planting, trimming, and making everything look just so. I used to tell her that if she tended to me half as much as she tended to that garden, I'd be the luckiest man alive. She would always respond by bringing me some freshly cut freesia and her sweetest kiss. It pains me some to think that she couldn't be given one last spring, even though she had the unique ability to appreciate each one as if it were her last. And for a moment, that thought stuck with me.

That is until Bill, the most joyful mailman alive, startled me with his vociferous "How ya doing?" He handed me the mail, and I just put it aside, too uncomfortable to look at who it was addressed to.

Well, it is getting late, and I'm awfully tired. I think I'll end for the night. Thanks for the ear, and thanks for being . . . a friend?

Oh, one other thing . . . I haven't felt this good in a long time . . . Thanks again.

March 8

How's it going, friend? I'm doing okay, although it appears I overdid it a bit last week. I was so enthralled with getting that yard in shape, I forgot how much it takes out of an old man like myself. So I've been soaking and resting and simply hanging around the house, watching the television and doing a little reading. The funny thing is I've been reading all these health magazines lately, and I thought I was on the same page as them, so to speak. Maybe not so much. Oh, well. Live and learn.

'Til we talk again . . . good night.

March 12

Friend, you're not going to believe what I did today. I was feeling much better and thought I'd start an exercise program. Those health magazines said it's never too late to take care of yourself. They even had an article about a fellow a bit older than myself. He was putting in over an hour per day of push-ups, sit-ups, and light weightlifting. He went on to say that he had only begun a year earlier when he was diagnosed with some health problems. And now his doctor has given him a clean bill. Of course, he suggests that anyone interested in beginning an exercise program should start with some easy stretching, so that's what I did.

I started with a few knee bends and some stretching, attempted a few push-ups, and then thought better of it. Believe it or not, I felt pretty good. So I did a little more and then called it a day. I'll see how I feel over the next few days and then make any needed adjustments to my routine. You know, I recall reading somewhere that maintaining a healthy body also improves your mind and vice versa. They said your whole attitude changes when you feel good about yourself. I figure, what have I got to lose?

March 14

Well, they say the second day is always the worst when it comes to being sore after a workout. I submit, they may be right, but I'm gonna survive. I may take another few days off, but then I'll have at it again. I think I'll adjust a few things and then give it another go. If the academy couldn't beat me, there's no way a few little stretches and bends are gonna. You know, friend, I think my attitude's improving already!

On another note, I hear the Giants are putting together a good group of young ball players. I love baseball season. I could watch it all day and review the box scores in the morning paper with great attention to detail to follow my favorite players and each team's standing. And I bet you'll never guess by the shape I'm in now that I used to be quite a snazzy third baseman, picking line drives in one fell swoop and throwing a bead across the diamond. I played for the Police Officers Union team. One year, they gave me the co-MVP award. I still think I should have gotten it alone. I recall hitting .415 with one homer, one triple, and a couple of doubles. I even drove in the winning run in the final game. But politics never cease. My co-MVP was the union VP.

Though I digress. I'll tell you there's nothing like those beautiful crisp white uniforms against the lush green grass and the burnt red infield dirt. Just thinking about it brings back that unique smell of the ballpark in the summer's heat. And nothing's as exciting as a comeback victory in the bottom of the ninth with two outs, runners in scoring position, and a three–two count. What a game!

March 19

Friend, this exercise stuff isn't as easy as I thought it was going to be. I barely completed my workout two days ago, and it's taking more out of me than I expected. My legs, my chest, and my arms feel like I got beat up. I'm so stiff and sore that I can feel every muscle in my body each time I rise or reach for my coffee. I was thinking, *Maybe I should talk to my doctor and get his opinion.* I am getting a bit older, and I'm hoping he would have some good advice as to how I should proceed. I'll let you know later what he said.

Anyway, I'm turning in early this evening. So . . . I'll just talk to you later. Good night.

March 22

Hello, friend. How's it going?

Today is the first day of spring. It was a beautiful day today. There was this buzzing in the air of great things to come. People seemed friendlier than usual, and the temperature nearly reached eighty degrees.

All in the world seemed right, yet I felt empty. I really missed her today. I longed to be beside her, walking hand in hand through the park. That was one of her favorite pastimes, when she could share her thoughts because she had my undivided attention. But the truth is my mind was never far from my work. She'd say silly things at times just to see if I was listening. But in the end, she tolerated me because she was just happy to be in the park, walking by my side. She used to love to admire the people from afar: the teenage lovebirds, the animal lovers, and, most of all, the children. Her face just lit up as she watched them run carelessly and aimlessly around. She'd talk about anything and everything while I just quietly walked beside her. What I'd give to share another walk with her right now . . .

I know. I can hear you telling me, "Stop the self-pity." And I can hear her agreeing with you. But seriously, don't you think I'm entitled once in a while to miss her?

Okay, okay, I'll cheer up. Tomorrow's a new day. But I think I'll go hold her robe for a bit before I turn in for the night. Until next time . . .

March 24

Hey, buddy. Not a lot to say, but just wanted to let you know I'm still alive. Sorry for leaving you with such a somber entry, but I think I'm doing better.

Oh, I almost forgot. I spoke to my doctor about the exercise program yesterday. The damn middle-of-the-road liberal told me what I could have figured out myself: "Don't overdo it. Take it slow, and your body will tell you when it's had enough." I don't know why I keep going back to him.

Anyhow, that's all I've got for now.

March 28

Friend, the weather changed yesterday. The rain clouds rolled in and painted the sky with dread. But it was more than an early April shower. As I lay in my bed, it felt like a lonely fall morning, with emptiness hanging in the air. The skies were much darker, and the little hope of morning anew quickly vanished when it seemed the thunder spoke directly to me. Its voice was thick and drew out every syllable, with canyons of separation echoing in its bass. It demanded my attention. Behind it, it seemed the rain and winds whispered and laughed at me from every corner of my room.

I was barely awakening and not completely sure of where I was or what was happening to me when I rubbed my eyes in an effort to clear my head. Yet nothing changed. The room grew darker. Gloom and doom began to immediately saturate the air. I thought about rising—at least, I think I did—but quickly succumbed and surrendered to the fog that now engulfed me. I felt trapped and chained to my bed. Though I didn't have the desire or strength to move. Gradually, inadequacy began to flood my mind as I felt as if someone handed me a burden that was beyond my ability to carry. I lay there futilely, drowning in my own misery.

At that moment, I was a failure, and there wasn't a thing I could do to think otherwise. My life had been one failure after another. I couldn't give her children. I couldn't save her life. I couldn't even bring her home to die peacefully in her own bed. My heart was heavy, and my mind's eye was flashing thoughts of destruction. I felt myself spiraling down into the deepest, darkest despair that I have ever experienced. No matter how much I tried to pull myself from its grasp, this growing despondence weighed on me. I remember asking myself why I was feeling this way, but I couldn't concentrate long enough to even remember my name.

I felt as if my heart was broken and it was reliving every personal tragedy it had ever experienced, all at that moment. I hurt so deep inside. I couldn't discern from where it originated. I was beyond melancholic. I was helpless and pathetic. I confess, I began to cry and, it seemed, for no reason at all. I wanted to just get up and slap myself back into reality, but I didn't have the energy.

So I lay there for hours, crying like a baby and being ashamed of myself for it. I circled in and out of consciousness, and I called to her for strength. I pleaded with myself to break free from whatever it was that had come over me. Though I was lost and I didn't have a clue as the walls began to close in on me. And I just lay there in a fetal position, staring at the television, while the morning news incoherently babbled on from some distant, faraway place. I was hopeless and so felt no or any reason for living . . .

Hours later, I awoke to a local auto dealer's jingle. I reached for the remote and eliminated the noise. As I lay there in the gray, murky silence, it seemed the storm was swirling around me, with the rain slapping at the window in waves. I looked at my bedside clock through heavy eyelids and realized that nearly half the day was gone. Then as I rolled out of bed and attempted to erect myself, it hit me like lightning.

My head was screaming, as if it were held in a vice that was, inch by inch, tightening. I quickly retreated to my knees, bent over down to the floor, grabbed my head, and wrapped myself in a ball. The excruciating pain radiated to the ends of each hair on my head and pulsated throughout my body. After several minutes and deliberate efforts to breathe lightly, I crawled my way slowly to the bathroom to relieve myself, thought better of leaving my room, and then, with much effort, made my way back to the safety of my bed.

As I lay there, nearly lifeless, terrible visions of death and helplessness returned. I cowardly retracted into my fetal position while clenching the blankets up to my chin.

Suddenly, something, a soft voice, was gently coercing me to end it all.

"Kill yourself," it whispered. "Go ahead. No one would care. Do it. Do it now, now, now," it repeated.

It told me that I was despicable, that I didn't deserve to live, and that the world would be a better place without me. And when my better judgment tried to interfere, the vice clamped even more. I was told that I was the cause of her suffering. I hated myself. Something inside of me was slowly invading my entire being and wouldn't be satisfied until I suffered a painstakingly tortuous death. I struggled with myself to think otherwise, but it was useless. I hated myself more than anything I've ever hated. Nothing else seemed to matter. There was nothing else to live for. No one cared, no one would miss me, and I deserved to die.

I went to the closet where I kept my old revolver, opened the case, and held the cold heavy iron in my trembling hand.

"Do it. Do it now," the voice instructed with a fevered pitch.

I could smell the scent of the burning powder from years gone by as I brought it up to my face. I looked at it with curiosity and held it without all the fear and respect it deserved. Placed the barrel in my mouth and closed my lips around it. As the tears ran down my face, I pulled the trigger. *Click* was the last thing I remembered hearing; then the gun and I dropped to the floor.

All time had ceased . . . and I gave in to the pain as it tore its way through my defeated heart. Blubbering, I eventually fell out of consciousness.

This morning, I awoke, surprised to be alive. I looked around with disbelief, shock, and confusion that I was still here in my own room. With the effects of the day before still lingering, I lay here on the floor, trying to make sense of the last twenty-four hours. Unsure if it had all been a terrible nightmare, I slowly turned my head while my eyes stiltedly scanned across the floor until they stopped and widened at the sight of the pistol lying there. Reality slowly sank in and then hit the pit of my stomach like a ton of bricks. I nearly vomited save for the lack of air, which was suddenly pinched off at my throat. And all I could muster was a strangled cough.

Nowhere in my darkest days had I ever before even considered such a dreadful act, and yet now I had to live with the thought that I had almost committed the unthinkable. And as my mind lost itself in that thought and the actual closeness I had come to death, suddenly, at that moment, I remembered, and I thanked her for never allowing me to keep the weapon loaded.

The storm had passed, and I resolved to turn my weapon over to the authorities, though fatigue and hunger had the greater immediate influence. So I made my way cautiously around the gun and into the kitchen to brew some coffee and toast some bread.

As I sipped at the hot rich black-and-amber liquid, sensation began to awake from its dormancy. My eyes became clearer, my olfactory senses opened, and my taste buds were graciously lapping up the bitter but welcomed flavor of an old friend. And though I felt like a budding flower on a spring morning, slowly reaching and extending to the warmth of the sun's light, somewhere deep within the covered earth, the interior of my seed was decaying.

I chose to remain confined for the rest of the day, not yet confident enough to confront the outside world. I sat in my recliner, watched the television, and learned that yesterday's storm was today's light showers and tomorrow's eastward problem. (And as I write this entry, I'm amazed they finally got it right.) Then they went back to the traffic problems and auto accidents of the midday commute, so I turned it off and sat there in the silence, staring out the window and watching as the periodic cars went swishing by. I tried to rest, closed my eyes, and attempted to take advantage of the bad weather, but instead, my mind tossed and turned, still engulfed by the recent events. Time passed as the rain tapped upon the roof with a mesmerizing rhythm. I felt alone. I felt abandoned. And I felt lonely.

Gradually, I cautiously approached the loneliness and brought it closer to me. As it began to permeate, I experienced its emptiness, forlorn and void. I felt its solitude, secluded and desolate, and I realized its sorrow, mournful and crestfallen. It was then that I laid down my shield, surrendered, and allowed the loneliness to penetrate deep into my soul. I embraced it and felt its intensity burn as a lifetime of heartache roared and moaned into capitulation, and I became one with its flame. Living within it, accepting it, and holding on to the pain—no longer afraid.

March 30

Crisp, clear skies made for a refreshing walk this morning. The streets and walks had a clean, damp aroma that reeks of better things to come. Days like these make you feel wonderful to be alive. As I strolled down the block, I took my time, simply admiring the neighbors' yards and appreciating nature's harmony.

The day didn't bring forth any thoughts of yesteryear, but instead, I lived for the moment. I hadn't even realized that I was free from my worries until this evening, when I became aware that I hadn't given a thought to . . . all the things that usually consume me.

What a way to live—without pressures, stresses, or deadlines. To utterly choose what the day may or may not be. Now that's real freedom.

I think I'll end on that sentiment. Good night.

March 31

Hey, friend. Today I hired the kid from around the block to cut the lawn weekly. He came knocking upon the door and had his mower with him, so I thought, *What the heck? I could use a little help.* But I'll tell you—these kids today, they don't come cheap. We had a little negotiation before I gave him what I was gonna give him anyway: five bucks for the front and five for the back. But he thought he made out.

Anyway, he appears to be a good kid, trying to earn enough money to buy a new skateboard. His name is Andy. I figured he couldn't be more than thirteen or fourteen years old. He had that awkward teenage look about him. No longer a child but not yet a young man.

So I watched him as he made his way back and forth over the lawn. Surprisingly, he did a very good job. He was neat, clean, and quick. It took him all of twenty-five minutes, what usually took me an hour and a half. Now that I think of it, the little businessman did schnook me. Anyway, he seems honest enough, and I really liked just having someone around, even if nothing but to entertain me.

April 3

Hello, friend. I was thinking about purchasing a computer with a word processor today. All this writing is beginning to look a little like hieroglyphics, and whoever reads this stuff one day will probably appreciate the gesture. I don't believe my penmanship is that poor, but then again, I know what I'm writing. I checked a couple of stores, listened to a few sales pitches, but I chose to wait and think about it a little longer. Besides, I feel a reader can probably get a better sense of a writer's feelings and personality if they read the long hand. Computers and typewriters have always seemed so impersonal to me, even when I had to use them in my report writing. You know, now that I think of it, that's probably why most awards and diplomas are written in old English—so it doesn't look like they just came out of the copier, even though most probably did.

Well, that's all for now.

April 6

Hey, friend. I've got a kind of silly question. Do you believe in karma?

The reason I bring this up is because I've been trying to figure out this crazy game we call life and, more specifically, my life. I know for the better part of my life, I've been a pretty fair, honest, and ethical man, but it's the times that I wasn't that have me somewhat concerned. I've tried to think back to all the things in my life that I regretted, and I'm thankful there haven't been many. But still, deep within me, I feel somewhere I've done something to someone that has taken me down the path I now am traveling. I can't, for the life of me, ascertain what it was, but it concerns me. Where I am today in my life is an ambiguous place. At times, I feel a great sense of accomplishment and peace, but at other times, I'm not so self-assured. I just wish I had the foresight then to realize the impact on today what my decisions of yesterday would have on my future.

As I sit here writing now, I am amazed at the amount of thinking life requires and how foolish I was to think it was all so easy. I always felt I processed information quickly and was able to make a decision. Maybe I didn't realize how much information I was discarding. It's hard to say. However, she was so good at taking the most complex things and breaking them down. She could explain things in such great detail or just give me enough of the cliff notes to satisfy my patience or rather impatience. And I can't understand how she was able to master all of this at such a young age. And maybe that's the answer to life's biggest question—life versus death. We come to understand the meaning, and then we must move on. I wonder how much more I have to learn.

April 15

Hey, buddy. It's been a while, and we've got some catching up to do, but first, I've got to tell you about my eye-opening day.

Now listen. You need to know that I'm not very religious, but I went to the Easter Sunday service today, just for old times' sake. The pastor welcomed me as if I hadn't missed a day. The truth is today was the first time I set foot on that holy ground in over a year. At first, I felt a bit strange, kind of out of place, and I wondered if anyone had noticed my absence. But then just as I found a seat near the rear of the church, the nosy Wilsons tapped my shoulder and kindly told me how nice it was to have me back again. I turned slightly, gave a courtesy smile and nod, and then turned back, feeling quite like the child who is surprised when his parent seems to always know what he's thinking.

Soon, the sermon began, and shortly thereafter, my mind commenced to wander as it always did when we'd attend together. You see, she would always have to remind me to pay attention or nudge me to keep awake. She knew I only came to satisfy her, but she hoped somehow I would pick up some of her faith through osmosis. (She was always the optimist.)

I could still hear the pastor's voice in the background, though my mind and eyes scoured the interior of the church as if it held some key religious secret deep within the crevices of the exposed wooden support beams and the white high-angled ceiling. I wondered if and where I too might find the faith that she so embodied. Yet what I found was so much more.

As I looked around at the congregation, I saw people for the first time, each different from one another yet all the same: young and old, rich and poor, healthy and lame, all yearning for guidance and understanding. They all weren't perfect; nor were they imperfect. They all weren't pious but most rather humble. Their wrinkled clothes, scuffed shoes, and hand-me-downs had never before been so obvious to me, yet now it really didn't seem to matter. Their "Sunday bests" were just that— the best they had. And although some dressed to impress, most were making their offering of the best they simply had. They were just like me, and I couldn't believe I had never seen that before—that is, seen who they really are and, more importantly, who I have been. There, in that building, we all were equal. Equally small in the greater picture, even if I hadn't quite fully grasped it yet.

Then before I left, I paused and thought about praying. And although it wasn't like me to talk to that which I didn't believe in, I sensed I was changing. So I reverently knelt and asked for forgiveness, just as she had taught me. I truly spoke from my heart, and oddly, I felt as if someone was listening.

As I left, this time, I didn't judge them so harshly or envy them as I had in the past. There was an acceptance that I found there. And that acceptance was not only of my fellow man but more importantly of myself and all that is. I realized we all had a burning need, and no matter how different that need is, it is equally compelling. Gradually, my heart began to feel one with theirs, beating collectively to the same drummer, filled with the same vulnerabilities, yearnings, and, most of all, hope. It made for such a blissful walk home.

I wonder—do you believe in God?

April 18

My good friend, baseball season is off and running. The Giants aren't off to a good start, but Barry looks like he's in the best shape of his life. He's hitting the ball out of the park regularly and looks like he's in for another possible MVP season. The rest of the team looks like they're getting younger by the year. We definitely need some pitching, but who doesn't? They lost today, five to three, but showed a lot of potential. It's a long season, so we'll just have to wait and see how things go. I'll keep you posted . . .

April 22

Friend, we had quite a scare today. The neighbors' house caught fire when the toaster shorted out. Thank goodness for the quick response from our local fire department, or they may have suffered extreme financial loss. Mrs. Barnes received treatment by the paramedics for the minor burns she incurred in her attempt to put out the fire herself.

Not to sound like a pyromaniac, but it was quite a show. The sirens and flashing lights reminded me of my days as a police officer. For a moment, my adrenaline started flowing, and I was looking for something to do. But instead, I ended up outside as an onlooker like everyone else on the block.

After it was all over, I went back inside and contemplated what I'd do if I had only moments to grab a few of my possessions in a fire. You know, the only thing that crossed my mind was to save you and my wife's diary. It's strange, when we are put in these situations, how quickly we determine what's really important—that is, outside of living. I guess what I'm really trying to say is I'm starting to depend on you . . .

This sounds crazy. Let me think more about this before I say something stupid. I'll talk to you later.

April 30

Friend, let's talk about where I left off last week. I've been trying to sort things out, and this is the only way I know how to explain it. I want to tell you about a partner I had in the department. His name was Frank Verducci. He and I were partners for fifteen years. He was the best cop I ever knew. I never told anyone this before, but if there was any other person whom I loved as much as my wife, it was he. Frank was a man of great integrity; he loved life, and he loved police work. He, unlike so many others out there, really felt he could make a difference. But more than that, he understood that he couldn't do it all by himself. He knew the importance of teamwork and the critical bond that partners needed to have with each other to survive.

We took care of each other's backs on and off the job. When my wife didn't understand what I was feeling, Frank did. When he was having problems at home, we'd spend the night in the patrol car, sorting it all out. I could tell Frank anything, and he could tell me anything, and there wasn't a single time that we weren't there for each other. That's how damn close we were. Other cops in the department would make fun of us, cracking jokes about our sexuality, but they were envious. They knew we had something special . . .

That's what I was trying to tell you. I'm beginning to feel like you've got my back. Like I can tell you anything. No matter how good or bad, you'll understand . . . and yet I can't go through this again. I can't allow myself to place myself out there again, and damn it, it's killing me. It's killing me, for Christ's sake! There's so much we need to talk about; there's so much I need to say. Please forgive me.

Listen, Frank committed suicide after his wife left him for another man. He was completely caught off guard. I would know; we talked about everything. He was completely blindsided. One day he's happily married and making plans to buy a vacation home, and the next, he's moving into an apartment where he finally decided he would end it all. You don't know for how long I hated her and then hated him for that.

Please don't misunderstand me; that is not what I'm thinking. I'm just reflecting on the only two meaningful relationships in my life and how they both ended. I know you can't die, but losing you right now would kill me. Even if we don't speak for days, I know you're there. I've come to rely on you . . . Friend, I depend on you like I did Frank, and that's all of what I was trying to say the other day.

Well, it's been a long day, and I have some thinking to do, so that's it for now.

May 5

Hey, buddy. It looks like the weather's warming up. I had time to bask in the seventy-six-degree sun today—that is, according to her old daisy thermometer hanging from the porch. I was just relaxing, reading the paper this afternoon, while Andy went to work on the yard. He's turned out to be a pretty proficient gardener and a good kid. He makes sure to pull the dandelions with his screwdriver he keeps in his back pocket, and he sweeps and cleans up any loose trimmings. He must have some really good parents. They seemed to have raised him with good old-fashioned values. He always addresses me as "mister" or "sir," even though I told him that he could call me by my first name. He just says, "Yes, sir" and goes about his work.

Other than a few questions here and there about the yard, he doesn't say much. But it's nice just having him around. I tried to give him an extra buck or two just to let him know that I appreciate his quality work, but he declined. He's a welcomed reminder to me that there still is good left in this world. My wife would have loved him. She would have made sure he took the extra money and left with some freshly baked cookies without taking no for an answer, even if she had to slip the money in a care package.

May 9

What do you think about "change"? I'm still working on this one, but I think perception and attitude are key.

I'll leave you with that thought for the night.

May 11

Good evening, friend, I picked up some things I needed at the grocery store this morning and decided to grab this jigsaw puzzle that was on the clearance table. (I know; what the hell is a jigsaw puzzle doing in a grocery store? I thought the same thing, but it caught my eye, and it was cheap, so I bought it.) I returned home and made myself a nice salami-and-mozzarella sandwich and jumped right into putting that thing together. I hadn't done one in years, so I figured it would be fun and occupy my time, particularly this one.

It was a double-sided puzzle with pictures on both sides of the pieces. On one side, it had a Coca-Cola bottle cap advertisement, and the other was the picture of those gambling dogs set around a poker table. That picture always amused me and reminded me of the days when a few of the boys and I would get together for the occasional all-nighter. I'd see the picture from time to time in stores and such, and I used to point out to her which dogs looked like whom, especially as the night and game progressed. She didn't find any humor in it; she couldn't relate, although the guys at work got a big kick out it. (I could still see their laughing faces.)

Anyway, I chose to put the puzzle together with the dogs' side up. It took me about hour to get the edges complete, and then the process slowed down to a crawl. Finding a piece seemed to be a matter of luck more than anything else. But it killed time and allowed me to pass the day. It also gave me more time to think about "change" and how important it is in life.

I'm a bit tired tonight, so I'll save that discussion for tomorrow, when my mind is much clearer.

May 12

Okay, where do I begin?

Let's start with the puzzle. I'll use that as an analogy. I spent another several hours today working on the puzzle. Initially, I was randomly picking pieces and attempting to find where they fit. I was searching and picking various parts and sections of the puzzle to work on and found that I was recycling many pieces I'd already inspected. Frustration started to build as I was going through the entire mound of pieces and wasn't getting anywhere fast. No matter how many times I sifted through the pieces and attempted to force an awkward shape into place, I returned to the same pile. Oh, sure, I did get lucky once in a while. But overall, not a lot of progress was made. As my frustration grew, I found that I wasn't enjoying this experience as I had hoped I would.

Finally, I got up and walked away from the puzzle to regroup and grab a beverage. I went to the kitchen, popped open a beer, grabbed a bag of pretzels, and conceded that I would have to change my approach. I was so caught up with the end result that I hadn't been thinking about the process. Eventually, I realized my stubbornness was getting in the way. So I reevaluated my approach to attain my goal. I changed my attitude and expectations. I settled in for what I realized was going to be a much longer endeavor. I placed all the like colors together, focused on a particular section of the puzzle, and began to sort each piece as I looked for the matching color and shape. At first, the process was tedious, but then I started to progress at a quicker pace. Soon, I had found that two or three pieces fell right into place, and I gleaned much satisfaction from this new approach.

My life hasn't been much different from this puzzle experience up until recently. All along, I kept the same attitude and perception of how things should be. I'd gone round in circles over the many things in my life and always felt the result was just a matter of how things were. I didn't take the time to step outside of my narrow little view and consider how things would be and could be different if only I changed my attitude and perspective. Now, after much contemplation and many years, I think the picture is getting clearer. Change is progress. Change is advancement. Change is growing. And above all, change is evolving.

I admit I became too comfortable with how I viewed the world. I used to think that Darwin said, "survival of the fittest," but I've recently learned that his actual statement was "It is not the strongest of the species that survive, nor the most intelligent, but the [ones] most responsive to change."

"Change"—such a simple and obvious concept, though to put it into practice often requires an act of God. I don't know if this enlightenment would have affected my past if I had known, and I'm pretty sure it wouldn't have. As for my frame of reference, being a cop meant surviving by being big, firm, and strong. But today I am a different person. And as I think back, I realize that the smaller guys were really the more successful, the more evolved. They didn't have the brute strength to bully people around. They used their ability to change and adapt to each and every situation they encountered as their mechanism for survival in law enforcement. It's no wonder many of them moved up the ranks so much faster than the rest of us. I was a dinosaur, and today many of those guys are extinct.

Today I look forward to every opportunity at learning something new. I enjoy learning and being informed. There are times I'll sit in front of that television and watch the craziest things. Even though I won't attempt half the projects they do, I still watch just for the education.

And I am changing, albeit at a pace comparable to a sloth. Even so, I realize I'm growing and I'm becoming more complete, like the pieces of my life's puzzle are gradually falling into place.

May 17

You'll never guess who stopped by today: the Branighans. Remember them? They were the neighbors who never tied their mutt down. They asked if I had seen their precious little Petunia. It seemed Petunia got loose again and this time didn't return. I almost rubbed it in their face and told them that I saw it coming, but I had a change of heart. I saw the look in their eyes and realized they were hurting. So instead, I asked for their number, told them that I would keep my eyes open and let them know if I happen to see her. Admittedly, it felt pretty good to turn the other cheek. Strange how life has a way of coming around full circle.

May 20

Nothing new going on around here these days. Just another lazy Sunday afternoon. I took a ride down to the local pharmacy to pick up a couple of prescriptions. Nothing much, just a few things to deal with some aches and pains. It's really been an uneventful day. I put some time into the puzzle as I had kind of pushed it aside for a couple of days. It's coming along. I'd say I'm between a quarter or a third of the way done. One and a half dogs down and more to go.

Andy was here yesterday. He did his usual great job with the yard but informed me that he would be giving his "two-week notice." He's such a considerate young businessman. He said he would be finishing school for the year and leaving for his father's house for the summer. I was surprised that he was the product of a broken home, though I shouldn't have been. Who isn't these days?

Well, those are the kinds of days of late—not a lot to talk about. Have a good night, my friend.

May 22

Hey, friend. Guess who turned sixty-three today? Yep, happy birthday to me! The funny thing is I didn't realize it until the morning news reporter blurted out, "Tuesday, May 22—a day to remember!" Then he went on to talk about the great rise in the stock market or something. It appeared that two individual companies each found some type of cure for rheumatoid arthritis. I listened for a while and then decided to treat myself to a little birthday gift.

I took a shower, cleaned myself up, grabbed my cap, my coat, and a blanket, and headed out to the ballpark. As I drove north to the city, the traffic moved at a comfortable pace. I had time to relax and listen to the pregame show. The Giants were beginning to play decent ball and had moved one game behind the second-place Rockies and three games behind the first-place Diamondbacks. But today's game was against the pathetic Padres, and not much was at stake. Though for me, it didn't matter who they played; it was just being there.

Highway 101 took me through the industrial part of the city and carried me right into the heart of San Francisco. As I was riding along through the heavy cement arteries, the view was like a postcard. As I entered the city, I was perched high enough to view the vast foreground of buildings upon buildings. Some cast in the sun and others biding for their moment. From a distance, the canvas reflected the intended beauty of the artist. Yet experience knew of the cold, impersonal shades of gray and shards of glass that made up the finer (or not-so-fine) details. Still, the breathtaking bluish-grayish-greenish San Francisco Bay in the background surrounded and lassoed it all in such a way that the picture was worth beyond a thousand words.

Soon, I was lowered into the midst of the shadows, and that transformation of attitude, which is more cognitive than not, comes to surface. Driving is no longer a privilege but a God-given right. And those who think otherwise are quickly indoctrinated or consumed. And with the amount of sign language (middle fingers) and horns blowing, you might think that everyone is hard of hearing. Eventually, you either come to hate this place or love it. For me, it's like a shot in the arm . . . I'm alive! Yet for her, she only tolerated the downtown in an effort to enjoy shopping at the Embarcadero wharf and piers. And the occasional ferry ride to Alcatraz.

I made it to the new ballpark just in time to catch the end of the national anthem. I picked up a Polish, some peanuts, and a soda, and I took my seat along the third baseline on the second deck. Soon, the players jogged out to their positions on the emerald diamond, and the first pitch was thrown.

"Steee-rike!" screamed the ump as I took a man-size bite out of my dog, and I was in heaven.

By the time the game had ended, the sun's bright light had only a dimming orange glow left to cast upon us. For the chilly San Francisco wind replaced any and all the remaining warmth left in the air. And the once-youthful, splashing bay now rolled with purpose as whitecaps lined up, waiting to take their turn at the wharf's piers.

Then before heading home, I walked down to the boat dock, stopped, and took one final gaze out across the east bay. The last of the sun glistened and skipped across the tips of the water as the western mountain range gradually laid its massive shadow upon the restless bay and kissed it good night.

The seals yelped and the seagulls cried as the piers and walkways emptied. I made my way out of the biting cold and back to the warmth of my car. Silence rang loudly as I pulled the door shut and escaped the stirring winds. I sat there a moment, reflecting on the amazement and simplicity of beauty and the wondrous of life while my bones slowly defrosted . . .

Then I started the car up and listened to the postgame show all the way home. It was a great birthday, even though the Giants lost.

May 26

Hey, buddy, tell me something—what do you think about fear? I'm not talking about irrational fear but real fear. Not fear of failure—but kind of? I'm talking about fear that goes beyond momentarily being startled. More than just fright . . . I mean being afraid and maybe even petrified beyond what's healthy. Kind of like . . . impending . . . fear, fear that builds as time goes on. Like you wrecked your dad's new golf clubs while hitting rocks on the driveway, and you know sooner or later, he's gonna knock on your bedroom door. That kind of fear, *real* fear.

Oh, forget about it . . . I'm just rambling again; I don't know what I'm talking about. There is just this sense, some uneasiness, that I've been dealing with. It even bothers me just to think about talking about it. Sorry I brought up the subject. Maybe on another night, we'll try this discussion again.

May 30

Tell me something, friend. Have you ever just sat and listened? I did this evening for about twenty minutes. I turned off the television, closed my eyes, and opened my ears. I tried not to think about anything I'd read or heard on the television. Instead, I lay down flat on my back and tried to hear whatever noise the outside world presented. Believe it or not, it was pretty quiet. So quiet that I felt a little uncomfortable. But I proceeded and concentrated on listening to my breathing. Soon, the silence of the outside world was nothing but a sheet of white noise, and calm entered my center. I was separated from the rest of the world by a thin layer of consciousness. I floated freely in my bubble, with only peace and serenity flowing through me. I'm unsure of the derivation of this feeling, for I only know cognitively, it registered and felt seamless or endless. And from what I can recall, time too was without measurement.

When I reentered my body, so to speak, I lay there for another five minutes or so. The white sheet disappeared and was replaced by the distinct humming of the refrigerator. I felt rested, but I also felt very weak, like somehow someone increased the gravitational pull, and simply raising my torso to sit up was a most arduous task. At that moment, I wondered if I had just experienced the difference between heaven and earth, life and death. And if I did . . . I am so glad she is there living in that peace.

June 20

Friend, I woke up a bit early and took my usual walk this morning after weeks of cabin fever, trying to fight off a persistent cough. Although dawn found me stiff and tired and time has a way of eluding my every desire to preserve it, I made my way outside and strode leisurely, observing the most beautiful part of the day. That is when most of Earth's creatures, including the crooks, are somewhere else, resting, and the world is a better place for those few hours.

The hidden virgin sun gradually illuminated the eastern sky, and I felt as if the early bird and I were the only ones on Earth as we witnessed the birth of the new day. Not a single car passed, and the air was clean, tepid, and calm. It was a perfect time to be one with nature before the riffraff awoke and the afternoon heat consumed the air. I could tell it was going to be another blistering day, the fourth one this week.

As I strolled down the block, my nose caught the scent of the neighbors' lemon tree before I actually reached it. I was immediately brought back to her sweet voice. You see, every time we'd pass it, she'd begin to sing that song. It was her favorite, and I could almost hear her singing as I walked—"Lemon tree, very pretty, and the lemon flower is sweet . . . La, la, la, la-la-la la-la . . ."

Well, I hummed it throughout my walk and couldn't get it out of my head the rest of the day. It is such a simple, carefree melody, much like her, although you'd never catch me admitting that to her. Yet I must own up: I kind of enjoyed it a bit too, especially coming from her voice. Though I believe she appreciated it even more, like when she'd catch me humming it on occasion. She'd kind of stop what she was doing momentarily. Then I'd catch myself, look up, and see her with her warm "I told you so" smirk. No wonder she liked it so much.

My stroll brought forth a peace that I hadn't been able to experience in quite a while. It also gave me much time to think about our relationship a little more. I didn't think I would be saying this, but somehow I knew that she'd be right. I have found that sharing my life and feelings with someone has given me the opportunity to contemplate, express, and cleanse my feelings. You have provided the ear that I have longed for. Although she is still and now ever so close to me, you have filled a great void. And I thank her for suggesting you to me, and I thank you for being there.

'Til next time . . .

June 24

Hello, friend. I sat on the porch for hours early this evening and

210

simply watched as the moon rose. The air was still and the temperature pleasantly comfortable enough to be without my sweater. You should have seen the size of the moon tonight. It slowly crept up from behind the mountains as if it were this monstrous jack-o'-lantern or gigantic grapefruit. It had never appeared so orange to me before. I could almost smell its tangy scent and taste its effervescence. Yet it rose so quiet and peacefully.

If I hadn't known what it was, I admit I'd feel a bit intimidated. But as it slowly ascended, its orange glow gave way to a more brilliant yellow, illuminating the neighborhood as if it were a huge streetlamp. Even as the glow radiated, it didn't obscure the detail of all the magnificent craters. I felt as if I could reach out with my hand and feel the texture with my fingers.

Eventually, it climbed to its rightful place in the night's sky and hung among the glittering stars as I gazed wonderingly at their significance and wished upon their majesty.

And though I know we've become best friends and I tell you almost everything, I can't tell you what I wished for for fear that it may not come true.

Who knows? Maybe later, I'll change my mind.

June 30

My friend, I believe I am learning to accept. Accept the changes in my life and try to grow from them. I know I can't start over, and I know I have a way to go, but I am looking forward to the changes upon my horizon. You wouldn't believe how freeing this feels. I've carried so much anger, guilt, fault, and shame for what seems like forever. Yet letting go and accepting that I am not in control is the most liberating feeling I could have never imagined only six months ago. It's crazy to feel this sense of evolvement. I truly feel like a ship that has had its anchor lifted. A wild stallion released to run free in the open field. A bird that has been freed from its cage. I tell you, there's no better feeling than how I feel tonight. Even my breathing is without the congestion that has been plaguing me. I can't wait for what tomorrow brings.

July 4

Happy Independence Day, friend.

It's been a couple of days, so before I begin, I wanted to let you know I completed the puzzle! Boy, what a feeling of satisfaction. I just sat there for a moment with a huge grin on my face when I placed the final piece. Then I stood up and just stared and smiled at it. I figured I wasn't ever gonna break it down and place it back in the box, so I went to the craft store and picked up some glaze glue so I can hang it up on my wall after it dries.

Today I spent the day sitting at the park, feeding the pigeons, and watching the children play. It was another hot day, reaching the low nineties, and the pyro-technicians were setting up for the evening bonanza. Fortunately, I found our favorite bench under the large maple tree.

I watched as the children chased one another with water balloons and was tenderly amused by their obliviousness to the rest of the world spinning around them. I thought, *How great it must be to be so young and free.* They hadn't a care in the world other than avoiding being struck. They were so full of life, and for a very brief moment, I envied them. I even secretly wished that one would run by and accidentally strike me with a balloon, just so I could see the light in their eyes. (Admittedly also to get a little refreshed.)

Then my thoughts turned back to the fall of '79. I had just received my lieutenant's promotion, and we were ready to begin a family. I recall how she desperately wanted to have children, and we spent many a splendid afternoon and evening giving it our best effort. But the months turned to years and the years to frustration. It just wasn't in the cards. We were both tested and pronounced fertile but apparently not with each other. I guess if there was one thing I regret not giving her, this would be it. She would have been the greatest mother . . . I should know. She often said I was her big baby. Yet over time, we adjusted, and she occupied her time volunteering countless hours helping out at the local shelter, organizing picnics and field trips. She loved those kids.

Which reminds me—you should have seen their faces light up during the fireworks show tonight. I'd have to say it was the most amazing production I've seen to date. The crowd was most pleased and impressed with the newest innovations. There was snapping, popping, whistling, and every color one could imagine. My favorite had to be the neon green and magenta rockets. The green exploded outward, while the magenta came gracefully spiraling down from the center. My eyes widened with the sheer amazement by it all. And I can still smell the unforgettable scent of the burnt powder still lingering in my nose.

Tonight I too felt like a child who was watching the fireworks show for the first time. I even got this miniature American flag to wave during the show. I held it up and waved it until the strength left my arms. I hadn't felt so much patriotism or had such exuberance in my heart as I did tonight. It sure is great to live in a country where we have the privilege to experience such wonders as I did this evening. Freedom—what a thought. It plagued me for so long; now it fills me!

And, friend . . . one other thing. I'll use this flag as a bookmark to remind me of and share with you the wonderfully breathtaking time I had.

July 7

Hey, friend. I know it's not like me to talk to you in the early morning hours, but I had a dream last night that has left me a bit shaken. I can't tell you how real it seemed. And yet I can't get it out of my mind.

Please believe me when I say she was here with me last night. She stood right beside me as I lay here in my bed. She was as real as the clock on the wall, though she appeared surrounded by this brilliant light. In all my deepest, heartfelt wishes of having her come back to me, I never imagined that it could happen. But I swear to you that she was real. She just stood there and smiled at me with a glowing, compassionate look in her eyes and held her arms out to me. I wanted to go to her, but I was paralyzed. I couldn't get up. I'm not sure why she came, but I believe I'm beginning to understand.

Friend, I've stalled long enough. There is something that I need to share with you. I haven't been completely honest. That is, I've been hiding something very personal. It's been on my mind from the first day I grabbed this pen, but it took until now to find a way to actually write it . . . to tell you.

Please forgive me for what I am about to say. For I am truly and sincerely sorry for how this will affect you. It was never my intention to deceive you or hurt you. But I could never find the right time to tell you. She gave you unto me, and you asked for nothing but honesty. You lay there and watched me with quiet integrity, keeping all that I shared in confidence. When I cursed you, you listened. When I cried, you comforted. And when I opened up, you didn't judge me. You surpassed any and all of my expectations. You have stood by me like she always has, and Frank would have loved you as much as I do.

You have been such a pillar of strength, yet I have failed you. I have failed to trust that I could fully lean upon you. And now that I will take this final step and place all that I am upon you, I am filled with guilt and shame over the selfishness of my behavior, for waiting so long and for the pain and anger that I know I will cause you. You don't deserve the way I've treated you, and yet I must accept responsibility . . .

So much have I learned from you, and still, as I write, so much am I continuing to learn.

My dear friend, please, please forgive me . . .

I'm scared. I've been scared for a long time. And I know the time is getting near. My friend, I don't know how to say this, so I'll just say it. I have cancer, and I am dying . . .

I've been in and out of the hospital for the past several months, and I am getting weaker by the day. They say it is only a matter of time. I can feel my lungs burning, and my breathing is becoming more difficult. Many a night, I have spent in the hospital alone, wishing I had you there with me yet knowing I didn't have the strength to write. I have been taking medication for the pain, but I told them that I didn't want the treatments they offered. I saw how she suffered—the slow, painstaking deterioration and the high-and-low roller coaster of emotions that we went through. Ultimately, I watched as the most precious person in my life curled up and took her final breath. She was brave. She was courageous, and she had perseverance. But that chemo took away the last bit of dignity that she so embodied. For me, I have chosen the easy way out. I will not be subjected to their cruel machinations and lie down for my final rest in some cold, sterile hospital room surrounded by strangers. This is where I belong and where she belonged . . . home . . .

I now know that she is truly waiting for me, and I look forward to that day with great anticipation. When we can be together again to share in all the happiness and love that made us so inseparable. It has been too long, and I am now ready.

So, my dear friend . . . if you don't hear from me again, please take solace in knowing that you have served your purpose. You have given me the opportunity to examine my life and appreciate all that has been and is. I am a better person for that. You have given my life the meaning that I lost and thought I would never find again. And you showed me that

I could be a sensitive, compassionate man—the young man whom she knew and loved. And for this, I am forever grateful and in your debt. Though I can't take you with me, all that you are, I will forever cherish in my memory and in my heart . . . and finally, I will miss our talks . . . Even though I've never heard your voice out loud, I'm sure it sounds like the angels . . .

July 8

Dear friend, the time has come. I can feel a tingling throughout my body. I can smell the scent of lemon blossoms, and I hear her beautiful voice singing to me . . .

This is truly my independence day. I will be free . . . Take care of my flag . . .

Lemon tree, very pretty, and the lemon flower is sweet, but the fruit of the poor lem . . .

February 19, 2001

I have come to realize that everything that was is. And everything that is will be.

Made in the USA
Las Vegas, NV
21 December 2021